GROW TO SUCCESS

A SET OF SKILLS THAT TAUGHT ME TO ACHIEVE PERSONAL AND PROFESSIONAL SUCCESS

ENAKA YEMBE

Success is not about wealth. It is not about the size of your bank account or your education. It is not about your age or position. Success is a personal sense of accomplishment, a feeling that you have succeeded in finding and accomplishing your God-given purpose.

To my beautiful and most cherished daughters, Ninche and Egbe. You both endured the test of time with me and have been and will always be the rocks of my life. In loving memory of my father, Dr. Omer Weyi Yembe, who inspired me and remained my lifelong mentor and confidant until he passed on to eternal glory in 2012 without the opportunity to read this book.

I am grateful to my mother, Mrs. Faustina Yembe, my hero. You got me to where I am today. Thanks, Mom, for patiently reading through this book and correcting my grammatical errors.

AUTHOR'S NOTE

All statements, tips, and strategies in this book are my personal opinion and a result of what has worked for me. Hopefully, these personal opinions and writings inspire you and grow you or your business to success. They are not meant to discourage or injure anyone, should they decide to act upon or reuse any information provided by me.

CONTENTS

Section 3: Perseverance

PREFACE

My primary mission is to *empower* individuals and organizations to gain the skills they need to *Grow to Success.*

I am the founder and CEO of American Stat Care Centers, a seven-figure medical clinic in Louisiana.

In 2006, less than a year after licensure, a medical emergency disabled me. What a blow! I was left without income for four and a half months. I was a licensed physician. I did not have any employment, but I had a dream. I chose to focus on my dream, build a plan, and put that plan into action. Working tirelessly and never giving up, regardless of the impossible odds I faced, I did it! I went from zero income with a credit score of 450 to owning a seven-figure corporation within eighteen months.

This book brings you several lessons and tips from my personal life experiences. Read carefully and refer to these tips often because that is how I took my passion of helping others and made it productive with perseverance.

Our busy practice, at the time I started writing this book, averaged about a thousand visits monthly. This has given me the opportunity to work with thousands of people from all walks of life over the past seven years. This, together with managing a multitude of full- and part-time employees and the John Maxwell Team training, offers unique and tremendous insight regarding what one must or must not do to achieve personal and professional success.

Imagine a single program that may potentially transform you and improve the quality of your life! This three-step program will provide targeted solutions to businesses and individuals who want to take control of their lives and create new, positive outcomes for themselves.

Are you ready to create to take your life to the next level? If I can do it, so can you. It's time to take control of your life, overcome all obstacles, and take yourself and your business to greater heights while maintaining the ability to foster what matters most to you: your relationships, yourself, and your future.

A famous quote says, "Choose a job you love, and you'll never have to work a day in your life." As early as the age of five, I knew I was destined to become a physician. Whenever asked, "What would you like to be when you grow up?" I always replied, "A doctor."

My journey has been a very long one, and with God's guidance, hard work, and sheer determination, I have succeeded in becoming a physician and an entrepreneur able to start three medical facilities in Louisiana (now consolidated into one).

I have been successful growing from nothing to owner of a seven-figure company that blesses others through the gift of giving.

"If you light a lamp for someone else, it will also brighten your path."
—Buddha

Today people, some friends and even family members, look at me and say words like "You are lucky. You have a great position. You need nothing." Any business owner or entrepreneur knows that there is no luck or good fortune about keeping a company up and running. It's nothing but hard work, consistency, determination, courage, staying focused, accepting failure, making changes, and simply keeping on with the grind.

The idea *Grow to Success* came to me as a result of following my passion of giving to others and bringing value to the lives of others. As a physician in practice for over seven years now, I have been privileged to see and be involved in over eight thousand patient visits. I have spent hundreds of hours counseling individuals on a one-on-one basis. I have been privileged to listen to and mentor individuals of all ages from many different walks of life.

This tremendous experience has been priceless to me and has helped me personally grow to success. The information you read here is a result of hundreds of hours of my personal experience at and away from work. And it is a result of attending multiple conferences with experts in personal growth and development and my encounters with thousands of individuals. I am also intricately involved in multiple sociocultural groups.

As a John Maxwell-certified team member, I have become experienced in a multitude of proven leadership and coaching strategies developed by the master himself of leadership: John C. Maxwell.

It is my desire and hope that this system will inspire you, empower you with knowledge on personal development, and ignite a burning flame that will take you from where you are right now, pick you up from your current position, and place you on the path to success.

Hold on tight! Read carefully, and take notes. Keep this book handy because it contains a lot of information that can take you by the hand and lead you step by step on your path to success.

ABOUT THE AUTHOR

I was born in Cameroon, West Africa. I am the second of five children born to well-educated, upper-middle-class parents. At the age of ten, I was enrolled into an all-girls Catholic boarding school. Sending one's child to boarding school in Cameroon in the 1970s was a prestigious thing to do. From my point of view, at the age of ten, it was nothing but the beginning of a terrible nightmare.

Every day we woke up at 5 a.m. at the sound of the bell, bathed in ice-cold water, and then went to church at 6 a.m. We followed a strict schedule implemented by the Holy Rosary Sisters; I simply counted my days to the next holidays when I got to leave the school and go home. Because I was a morbidly obese child, weighing about two hundred pounds by the age of ten, I had a lot of sad days. I had almost no friends in school. I felt I was a misfit. There were days when I was made fun of. Days when I felt left out. But like everything else in life, within a short span of time, I got used to the drill of boarding school life. I performed well in school and, unknown to me at the time, developed a lifelong, cherished bond with my schoolmates.

After my first three years in boarding school, my father got transferred to London. My age (thirteen) in England was considered too young to be placed in the grade I had attained in my country, which was form four (tenth grade), so I was actually placed back into form three. After one year in England, my parents sent me back to the same boarding school, Our Lady of Lourdes, a situation I was not happy with because my classmates were now a year ahead of me. Anyway, I survived boarding school and, in the process, had instilled in me many Christian attributes—discipline, purpose, and resilience—that have pulled me through many trials and tribulations of life.

After high school, I left my country at the age of eighteen armed with an unwanted (to me) government scholarship and went to Nigeria to complete a bachelor's degree in biochemistry. I earned a Bachelor of Science degree in biochemistry in the University of Lagos. I struggled with my weight because I was still morbidly obese. I hated biochemistry and felt it was terrible that I had to major in a discipline which I had no interest in and actually disliked, simply because I was awarded this government scholarship. I wanted to become a doctor. That was my dream from early childhood. So after my stellar performance at my first degree, I was automatically awarded a scholarship to pursue a master's degree in biochemistry. I declined. I became one of the few Cameroonian citizens to decline a government scholarship. So here I was at twenty-one: weighing at least 280 pounds, without a job, and with a bachelor's degree in a discipline that I hated. Amazingly, none of my family members realized how miserable I was on the inside.

My passion was in medicine. I did not want to waste any more time studying stuff that I did not care about. I struggled to find a medical school for myself inside and outside of my country. My initial start at medical school in Monrovia, Liberia, was thwarted by the gruesome Liberian civil war. So at the age of twenty-two, and slightly over three hundred pounds by this time, I was back home in Cameroon, feeling lost in my own country. I dreamed of becoming a medical doctor and had two options: go to Europe or to the United States.

I moved to the Universita Degli Studi di Milano in Italy for my medical training. As a medical student, life was very difficult. I had to study as well as communicate in the Italian language only. I also experienced a major culture shock. At the age of twenty-three, I realized that I needed to be employed to assist my parents in paying my way through school. I started off by braiding hair for the first two years. During the last four years of my medical training, I was blessed to have a full-time job; I worked as a night nurse to an elderly lady from Monday through Saturday and went to school during the week. I was off every Sunday. Even though my routine was mentally and physically challenging, I earned stellar grades with a magna cum laude in several courses and graduated from medical school in record time.

I then relocated to the United States to further my education, and in 2005, I became board-certified in family medicine.

About a year after graduation, I was faced with a medical emergency while working as an emergency room physician and ended up undergoing surgery. I was placed on bed rest and then was off work for four and a half months. This was one of the most difficult times of my life. It was mentally, physically, financially, and emotionally challenging. I often wondered what would become of my two daughters and me. I spent a lot of time praying and meditating and was extremely depressed by the possibility of never being able to work again even with all the education I had secured.

After the first two months of bed rest, I started to dream about creating a stand-alone medical facility for medical urgencies that would offer immediate care to the population, offer jobs to others, and allow me to work from home in an administrative capacity. This was because my recovery from this medical condition was unpredictable; after thirty days of being confined in my room, I had started to worry that I may not be able to get up and about, talk less of holding any gainful employment. Therefore, from my sick bed, which I had nicknamed "the command center," I researched and designed American Stat Care Centers. I hired a consultant to guide me through the process as well. It was overwhelming. I had no money, had two children to support, and had a very expensive project design on my hands. I struggled to get a bank loan, and every day I was turned down. I started to get depressed again. However, I prayed a lot during this time, and it was with the help of God that my attitude and my mood turned around. I came across the following quotes:

> "It is our attitude at the beginning of a difficult task which, more than anything else, will affect its successful outcome."

—William James: An American philosopher and psychologist often referred to as the father of American psychology. (1842-1910)

"You can commit no greater folly than to sit by the roadside until someone comes along and invites you to ride with him to wealth or influence."
—John B. Gough. A public speaker, known for his lectures against the evils of alcohol. (1817-1886)

One day, about four months into bed rest, I decided to drive down to our local bank. This was the first time I had driven since my surgery. I believed in my business plan. I was convinced it would bring a much-needed service to the population. My plan was approved.

My idea became alive, very slowly, because my funds were limited. I became knowledgeable in how a building is constructed. I read books on construction, met with the architect, actually took my building plans to the home improvement retail stores, and learned more about what it takes. I knew what licensed specialist was needed at the various times of construction. I visited several auction sales, yard sales, and different kinds of sales to obtain cheap equipment for my facility. Needless to say, the clinic construction was very cost effective, eventually opened in a short time, and was of immediate service to the people.

The first American Stat Care clinic construction was rapidly followed by three more constructions and then consolidation into one clinic that is now fully operational. Patients are free to walk into the clinic at any time and are always amazed at the quality of care they receive and at the quality of these facilities and the extensive nature of testing they can receive quickly. American Stat Care Clinic, at the time this book is written, has a patient load of about 14,500 contact visits a year.

I am actively involved in medical education by serving in the LSU Family Medicine Residency program at E.A. Conway Hospital, Monroe, Louisiana. I also serve as a clinical training instructor for medical students from LSU Shreveport and for those from surrounding-area nurse-practitioner programs and medical-assistant programs.

As a certified John Maxwell team speaker and coach, I am an inspiring, informative, and dynamic speaker whose primary mission is to empower entrepreneurs to gain the leadership skills they need to run and grow successful businesses.

As owner and CEO of American Stat Care Centers, a seven-figure medical clinic in Louisiana, I have developed a very solid and practical understanding of what business owners must do to run successful businesses and what individuals must do to sustain themselves and stay focused on their goals and dreams.

A leader in several sociocultural groups, I have also completed multiple speaking engagements over the past five years to audiences small and large, and of all ages.

STEP 1: PASSION

"A Great leader's Courage to fulfill his vision
comes from passion not position."
—John Maxwell

Passion has been defined as "boundless enthusiasm" or "the object of enthusiasm. *Merriam-Webster's Collegiate Dictionary* describes passion as a strong feeling of enthusiasm or excitement for something or about doing something.

GOALS

The online dictionary defines a goal as the object of a person's ambition or effort; an aim or desired result. I will put emphasis on the phrases "ambition" and "desired result." This definition focuses on the emotional aspect and an end in mind. You must have an end in mind. You must find your "why," a reason why you want to achieve this goal. In order to be successful, you must be crystal clear about your goal and then make a plan to achieve it.

So let's start with a few questions. What is the object of your ambition? What is your purpose? What is it that you are most enthusiastic about? What is that one thing or set of things that keeps you awake at night or wakes you up early in the morning? And why are you passionate about this goal? What is your purpose in life? How do you find your purpose? How do you stay passionate about your goals and your dreams? How do we make these goals and dreams a reality? I know! So many questions! I'm trying to impress upon you the importance of thinking. If you are not thinking about your goals and your dreams, then make every effort to activate your brain and start this thinking process.

Not only is it important for you to know what your goals and dreams are, as well as for your goals and dreams to become a reality, it's also important that this goal or dream adds value to be of service to your life and to the lives of others.

I had the idea of opening a clinic before I finished my residency training. Even though after my graduation I experienced a major setback with illness,

I was convinced that I would succeed in realizing my dream. This was because the clinic would offer open access to everyone. Typically, patients have to make an appointment to see the doctor. The idea of a walk-in clinic was literally unknown in Monroe, Louisiana, where I lived. The value this facility would bring to the local population was unquestionable.

Right from the beginning of the clinic's operations, I made up my mind I would employ local people. Therefore, from services offered to employment opportunities, the clinic was structured in a way that it would bring value to the local community.

Giant corporations like Walmart focus on their products and services; however, they also have a strong philosophy of giving back locally. Walmart has a Volunteerism Always Pays (VAP) program through which the Walmart Foundation awards grants to eligible organizations where associates volunteer. In 2012, Walmart associates volunteered more than 2.2 million hours and generated more than eighteen million dollars in local grants through the VAP program.

In May 2013, the Louisiana State University AgCenter 4-H program received $65,000 of a two-million-dollar grant from the Walmart Foundation to help teach healthy living and eating choices. The grant helped 4-H implement its third year of the program, Fit4TheFuture. The program will be conducted by 4-H teen leaders along with adult volunteers and 4-H agents.

I give you these examples just to drive home the message that your goals and dreams should add value to others' lives in order for you to be successful.

What if you haven't even figured out what your goals and dreams are? What if you have several thoughts on this and feel like going in all directions at the same time? Wondering how to zero in on what your true passion or calling in life is?

Wondering where to start? Take inventory of where you are right now. The book *Acres of Diamonds*, by Earl Nightingale, teaches us a timeless story: each of us really is right in the middle of his or her own acres of diamonds, if only we have enough sense to realize it and develop the ground we're standing on before we go charging off looking for greener pastures.

Here's a system I've used to zero in on a new goal or dream.

1. **Desire**

   What is the object of your desire? Spend some time thinking about it. Spend some time alone thinking about the object of your desire. Where are you in life right now? Evaluate yourself and your circumstances and begin from there. What specific ideas fit the image of your desire?

   From the day I was born, I wanted to become a physician. I don't remember any encouragement from family or friends. It is just what I wanted for myself. My desire was so great. as a young teenager, not only was I very fascinated with the human body, I decided on my own to follow my aunt and my mentor who was an ophthalmologist to the hospital to watch her work. By the age of sixteen, I was very familiar with the operating room because I watched my aunt and her colleagues perform various surgeries.

   Next, dream big, but don't exaggerate. Setting goals that are outrageous are a way of setting yourself up for failure. I decided to start my clinics from nothing. It was a big dream but not outrageous for my circumstances, so I persisted and forged forward. I succeeded. Make sure your goals and dreams are attainable.

2. **Results**

   Next think about the results that you hope to achieve. This is your "why." Focus on the results that are most important to you. These results will be the *driving force* behind the burning flame of your passion.

   Once again using my clinic as an example, I had a few reasons why the clinic was set up the way it was initially. I wanted a facility where people could walk in at freely without having to wait for several days for an appointment. I was convinced, and this fact has been documented as true, seeking care in the emergency room for non-emergent care is not only a waste of time and costly for the patient but also a waste of time for the emergency room resources. I wanted a facility that could operate even if I was not physically present on site. These were my two biggest whys.

3. Inventory

Remember your goal, dream, or passion should start with where you are. So you have to make a thorough assessment of yourself. Don't explore completely new avenues that are unfamiliar territory for you when you may achieve more by growing the skill that you already possess. As you will read further in this book, commitment is one of the keys to success, and you cannot be committed to goals that are completely unfamiliar to you.

4. List

I find that writing things down helps me think them through. It also saves my thoughts. So a good way to start is to make a list of at least ten things you are passionate about. Dream *big*. Take about five minutes to quickly list these ten things.

In the summer of 2013, I decided to become a motivational speaker. I remember clearly I was having a conversation with my practice manager and a gentleman who was to become my web designer. He described details about what the practice website he was to work on would look like. At a certain point, he looked up at me and said, "You can insert a link to your speaking website here." I laughed and said, "I'm not a speaker." He looked at me surprised and said, "Oh, I assumed you were one. Well, if you are not a speaker, you should become one." Still very amused but intrigued, I explained, "Well, I have spoken in several capacities and to different audiences for at least five years now." Anyway, to cut a long story short, after spending some time thinking about this, I decided I would become a speaker.

Next came the dilemma of exactly what my niche would be. This is when I started to make a list of speaking topics and followed the exercise you see here.

5. **Passion**

Pick the top five goals you are most passionate about. Make sure these things fit you and no one else. You may discuss these things with a mentor. It's important to be mindful of the people you choose to share your thoughts, your goals, and your dreams with. Be aware that some people closest to you will scoff at you and advertently or inadvertently quench the dreams you have and kill your passion. Don't let this happen. Be courageous. Think of the value of this goal and dream and what it will enable you to do for yourself and for others.

6. **Clarity**

Spend more time thinking about these top five goals. Get crystal clear about the results you hope to achieve. Refer to these results periodically and often, for they will keep you on track with your passion.

If you are not quite clear or hesitant, just move the goal to the bottom of your list and focus on the top ones, but keep moving forward so you don't remain stuck.

7. **Courage**

One of the biggest myths is that success comes because of luck. Oh no! You may forget luck. You may forget even preparedness. In my point of view, success comes because of a multitude of different things which *together* lead you to success and then you must work hard to maintain it. Success comes because of hard work, courage, consistency, ingenuity, and courage.

You must be bold and courageous in order to succeed. Each of us was born with the God-given ability to achieve success. So by birthright, you have the power to succeed just like anyone else. So don't be intimidates by the word success. Stop thinking about your fears: fear of failure, fear of change, fear of disappointment. Eliminate the fear factor. Right now, think only about *what* this passion or goal is.

8. **Reflect**

You fill be surprised how easy it is to fall into life's busy schedule without really spending time to put any constructive thinking into our goals and dreams. Thinking is a very important habit to cultivate. Thinking before acting will help steer you in the right direction as well as save you time, energy, and resources.

Note: prayer and meditation help. Make sure your thoughts are in line with your core values.

Well yes, my Christian values play a part in who I am and what I do. I pray to God when I need guidance, as well as at other times.

9. **Emotions**

Don't think of *how* to make this dream a reality. Instead, think about how you will feel once your goals and your passions become a reality.

Our emotions are key driving forces behind the reasons why we do what we do. I have a few reasons why I have the zeal to help others. One of the reasons is because it is such a wonderful feeling for me to be able to lend a hand to another person. It's also one of my callings, so it's my second nature to help others.

10. **Focus**

Focus on the value of your goal. Don't be ashamed to ask for help or have this discussion with an expert, a mentor, a leader.

Cherish your visions. Cherish your ideals.

Cherish the music that stirs in your heart, the beauty that forms in your mind, the loveliness that drapes your purest thoughts.

For out of them will grow all delightful conditions, all heavenly environment, of these, if you but remain true to them, your world will at last be built.

—James Allen, *As a Man Thinketh*

11. **Authentic**

Spend more time thinking about these top five. Be sincere with yourself. Be authentic. Most people have a health goal, a financial goal, and a relationship goal. I had a lifelong professional goal. I have stated here that I've always wanted to be a physician. Keep in mind I was a little girl growing up in Africa. At that time, I knew nothing about power or position that may come with the title. Being a physician was simply the deep-seeded, authentic object of my ambition.

12. **Plan**

Now that you have set your goals, get ready to make a plan to achieve these goals. Be intentional about this and work on your plan daily. Don't be rigid about your plan. Evaluate your progress often, and modify or improve on it as you go along.

In figuring out what your goal is, start with some soul searching. Look into your innermost desire. Ask yourself what result you expect. Are you passionate about it? Activate your brain and reflect on your goals. Be clear and passionate about it. Lastly, design your plans to achieve your goal. Plans are essential, can be modified, and should be evaluated often. We will talk about planning later on.

A common acronym used in goal setting is SMART, which has evolved to the SMARTER criteria. SMART stands for **specific, measurable, attainable, relevant,** and **time-bound.** SMARTER **stands for specific, measurable, attainable, relevant, time-bound, evaluate,** and **reevaluate.**

Let's examine each of these criteria.

Specific

We must make every attempt to be specific about our goals and our dreams. You must be crystal clear about what you hope to achieve and why.

Measurable

Unless you can measure the progress of whether or not you are making progress on your goal, you may now be able to achieve it. So your goal must be measurable.

Attainable

As we mentioned earlier, set realistic goals for yourself or for your corporation. It's a good idea to set high goals so that you stretch a little. However, don't set them so high that you break while trying to achieve them.

Relevant

Set goals that are relevant to you, your team, and your business. For example, I am a physician and a family practitioner. I cannot set a goal to perform one hundred cardiothoracic surgeries before the end of the year. That kind of goal is unrealistic for me, irrelevant to my practice, and unattainable because I am not a surgeon. Though that's an extreme example I used to drive the message home.

Time-bound

Finally, we talk about when. Set a deadline and commit to it. This will help you stay focused and stimulated to meet your deadline.

Evaluate

Go back and look at your goals on a regular basis. Be adaptable to change. It's critical to be flexible because life around us changes often so we should be able to adapt accordingly. So looking back at your goals to make sure they are in line with where you are is important.

Revaluate

Repeat the process.

Let's simplify the concept and look at a visual. Visualizing concepts with simple drawings and diagrams helps simplify things for me. I use a lot of sketched drawings to help my patients understand what I'm explaining to them.

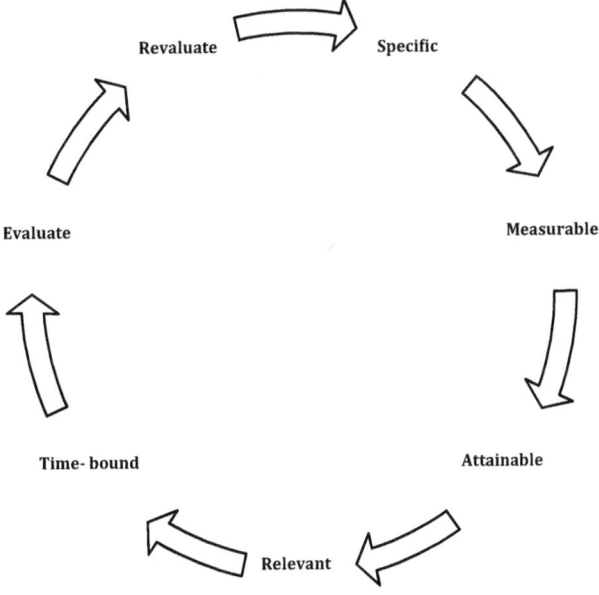

When it comes to the goal and mission of an organization, it will take a leader to guide and direct the team toward successful accomplishment of the goals and the mission.

Leaders typically have the emotional drive and their goal-driven mind-set to keep them focused on achieving success. Leaders have the ability to defy personal fears, accept unavoidable difficulties, overcome sociocultural obstacles, and set higher standards in order to achieve what they set out to accomplish.

A leader is not only the one who just holds this position but is the one who has the ability to influence the entire team toward the accomplishment of the organization's goals.

Some important qualities of a good leader include

1. Vision
2. Knowledge
3. Commitment
4. Integrity
5. Being goal driven
6. Being consistent
7. Focus
8. Courage
9. Empowering others
10. Being a people person

KNOWLEDGE ACQUISITION

Now that you have figured out what your goals and dreams in life are, your next step should involve the purposeful acquisition of the knowledge and skills that you need to understand the basics of accomplishing this goal.

You also need to invest in yourself in order to place yourself on a path of continuous learning. This will give you a solid foundation and skill set on the intricacies of your goals and dreams. You cannot outgrow yourself. So you must expand your knowledge in order to grow. Without knowledge, you would simply be walking in the dark.

Knowledge is undoubtedly one of the most important ingredients needed for peak performance. In order to be good at anything, you must acquire, maintain, and repeatedly refresh the knowledge in what you choose to do in order to do it well and to keep up with the rapid changes that occur in our times.

From the day I was born, I wanted to be a doctor. In order for this dream to become a reality, I had to go through the formal education process. I completed a four-year undergraduate education, the six years in medical school, and another four years in graduate medical education. The process will vary from individual to individual.

Assuming you choose not to go through a formal lengthy educational process, you must understand that getting skilled at anything takes time. This puts us all at the same beginning level so no matter what you chose to focus on, you must invest the time to master it.

We now live in a world in which technology is rapidly changing and becoming more and more sophisticated. The impact of technology on work and wages is still controversial. However, it is almost apparent that technology has

- increased skill demand
- improved productivity
- increased transparency
- streamlined processes
- increased wages
- advanced global thinking

Knowledge acquisition as well as personal growth and personal development are vital attributes needed for success. Personal growth and self-awareness enhance quality of life and contribute to the realization of goals and dreams. Knowledge acquisition is not limited to personal development but also includes formal curriculums for professional development.

Napoleon Hill, author of the famous book *Think and Grow Rich*, said, "Whatever the mind of man can conceive and believe, it **can** achieve." This is means it's not about the information that you receive. It's about what you do with this information. This means that you must be willing and able to use the information and the knowledge that you will have acquired. Keep in mind that even the best-educated people continue learning and absorbing more knowledge from several sources and at every opportunity.

Here are ten steps that help me acquire knowledge:

1. **Expose yourself to knowledge.**

   Read books, journals, and information from other sources that enhance your personal knowledge.

2. **Control your input.**

   Be careful about the information that you allow yourself to receive. Don't clutter your mind and your thoughts with overwhelmingly negative input.

3. **Research** and spend time studying where to get information that is useful to you.

4. Make an effort to *acquire knowledge daily*. That human mind learns by repetition. Knowledge cannot be acquired in a day. But lasting knowledge takes continuous and sustained periods of learning. I have made it a habit of listening to a personal development seminar for thirty minutes to an hour daily.

5. **Spend time thinking.**

    I agree with James Allen, the author of a *As a Man Thinketh*, who said, "A man is literally what he thinks, his character being the complete sum of all his thoughts."

6. **Develop a positive mind-set.**

    Too much negativity can limit or interrupt your thought process and reduce, limit, or impair your ability to become successful.

7. **Work hard and work consistently.**

    Do not expect a personal development or success process to be an easy feat. Darren Hardy, the founder and editor of *Success* magazine, teaches, "No pain, no gain!" You have to learn to push yourself past the limit of pain, and after your pain limit, the reward increases drastically.

8. **Time management** is one of the keys to success. You must learn to manage your time wisely. Some studies show that the human mind can focus only for up to ninety minutes at a time. I have trained myself to stay focused on the task at hand for sixty to ninety minutes, then take a break, and then repeat the process until the task is completed.

9. **Invest in yourself.**

    A good rule of thumb that I have learned over time is that one should invest 10 percent of one's earnings on oneself, 10 percent give to charity, and the rest goes to one's leaving expenses and savings.

10. **Listen and observe**.

Attentive listening and keen observation to the events around you will enhance and improve your knowledge capacity.

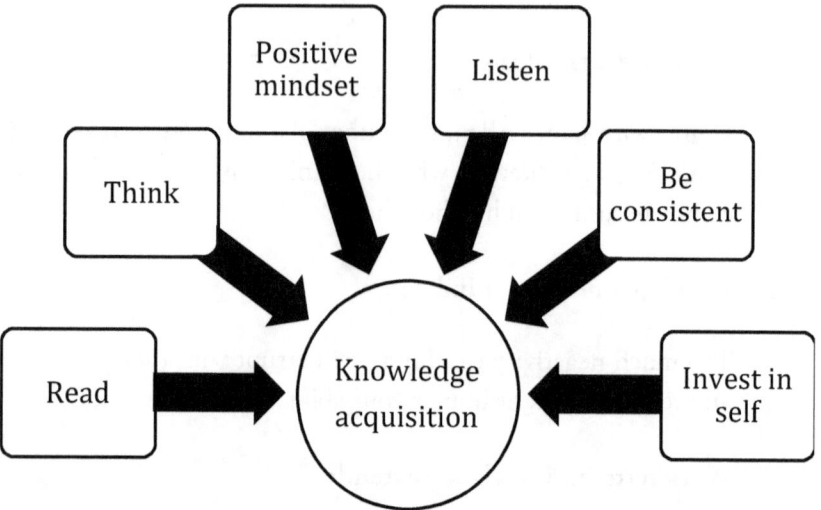

Specific Knowledge That Helped Me Lead My Business to Success

1. **Skills set.**

Every leader must have the skills in the specific field or industry. They must be able to bring into the organization team members that possess needed skills that the leader may not possess. A good leader must embody the behavior they expect to see in the rest of the team.

I am a family practice physician. In order to become one, I had six years of medical school training and then another three years of training in a family practice residency program.

As an owner of a medical business facility, I made up my mind very early in the life of this business that I would spend a certain amount of time learning some of the different aspects of the practice itself. So I learned how the X-ray machine works. I learned about medical billing and coding.

Other specific skills, such as taxes, accounting, and medical law, I did not study. To me, these specific skill sets must be outsourced to a specialist.

2. **Teamwork.**

   No two team members are same or have the same ability or skill set. So a good leader should understand the strengths of each team member and fit them in the position where they can personally and professionally grow and excel.

   Again, using the example of my practice, I have some front-desk personnel who are also trained and certified medical assistants. These can easily fill in positions in the front office and in the back office with the nurses. I also have front-desk personnel who have no nursing skills or training. These remain in the front, for it is where their strengths lie. I do not try to train them in the back office.

3. **Be adaptable to change.**

   The leader must be flexible enough to let in new ideas and concepts brought in by the team members.

4. **Time management training of the team** is another marketable skill that is a must have and taught to the team members.

5. **Be a good leader.** A good leader shows the way. To lead the team, you must be able to "get in" and show that team. In my clinic, I purposefully trained myself in all practical aspects of the business so that I am able to understand and provide meaningful advice when I meet with each department head.

6. **Analytical thinking**. The leader should be able to think in a critical manner and solve problems in a constructive manner. I think while sitting on my throne. I know this sounds crazy, but my throne is my toilet. It was very important for me to have a throne in my office as well. So when I constructed my newest clinic, I installed a handpicked toiled inside of my own bathroom attached to my office. This is where I can sit alone when I need to think and remain undisturbed. You find a thinking spot that works for you.

7. **Create other leaders.** This is one of the most vital skill sets you must acquire knowledge in. An organization that is made of people who possess the best skills will not flourish if it is not led appropriately.

   In my company, for example, we have excellent people. Phenomenal personnel who bring their best to work every day. I find that even though everyone works diligently, policies and procedure set even six months ago are just not followed as thoroughly and things tend to slacken as time goes along. When that happens, the leaders regroup, reinforce things, get everyone's input, come up with a game plan, and then move ahead with renewed vigor. Note that the skills of the individual team members did not change. In fact, their skills improved because in a medical facility like ours, the more often you perform a procedure, the more skilled you get. But the follow-through on other business matters slackened up, and that's where their team leader came in, redirected, and reinforced, and things became smooth sailing once more.

PLAN

The *Wikipedia* dictionary describes a plan as any diagram or list of steps with timing and resources, used to achieve an objective. It is commonly understood as a temporal set of intended actions through which one expects to achieve a goal.

Why plan? You may be asking yourself this question. You've figured out what your goal is. You have acquired the knowledge. Why plan?

Trust me on this. Not planning your steps to achieve your goal can cause you to get derailed repeatedly and, in the end, you risk missing your target!

Before I built my first clinic, I had gained the medical knowledge and skill to practice family medicine. In order to secure a bank loan, I had to write a business plan, which told the bankers what, how, and why I was to proceed with my plan and what I hoped to achieve.

I will share an excerpt of the business plan I used in the spring of 2006 to apply for a bank loan. Note how precise and clear my start-up plan was. I call this "The plan within the plan." It starts by describing the location of the facility.

> "The facility will be a stand-alone building within a small office complex setting. The building faces a heavily traveled street, which provides signage for automobiles that pass by each day …

Then it describes the services.

> "My goal is to provide premier urgent medical care and minor surgical services … for people unable to conveniently and timely receive medical attention from emergency facilities or their regular health care providers."

I then describe my reason for choosing a specific location, citing specific evidence based on statistics and physician shortage data, the competition, and a SWOT analysis specific to my business model.

I also had a specific marketing plan.

> "The basic marketing approach is to eliminate barriers of entry in order to allow all patients who seek services at the urgent care center to have access to it. Contract with all commercial insurance plans. These insurance plans can notify all their members of the "Urgent Care Option" for non-emergent, urgent illnesses which cannot wait for their doctor to be available the next day. A simple mass mail-out will accomplish this need.
>
> Organize health fairs in schools for sports physicals. Contact nurse case managers and give lectures beneficial to their various areas of specialty. Billboard advertising. Visit local businesses to develop occupational health business. Design brochures for handout and direct-mail utilization. Target areas based on zip code, sex, and income for direct mail pieces. Target newsletters for community areas. Go directly to physician offices and introduce the practice and physician. Go directly to hospital departments and floors to introduce the practice. Conduct an open house for physician and office staff. Conduct an open house for public."

The plan also included specific details on ownership, office management, a financial plan, and a two-year pro forma.

Organizational Matters/Ownership

The urgent care clinic will be owned by a yet to be incorporated company that will be set up as a LLC. I will be the sole owner, but as the clinic develops in the future, it is foreseen that other physicians will be welcomed as partners.

Office Management

The consultant will assist me with all operational concerns, the hiring of staff, and developing of administrative protocols. Healthcare facilitators will also on an ongoing basis assist me with strategic development and the marketing of services.

The clinic will first hire office manager with experience in urgent care setting. The manager will have multitask responsibilities for billing, supply purchases, and some clinic assistance. As clinic increases in volume, additional staff will be hired to assist in clinic tasks.

Financial Plan

Please review attached two-year pro forma with explanation of revenue calculations, patient projections, and expenses. This also includes projected start-up, staffing, and capital budget projections.

So as you see above, even before I leased a gray shell, I had a detailed plan in mind on the necessary steps what I would need to take to make this idea come to life. I had also done an extensive amount of work comparing costs and purchasing equipment. Working with the contractor, I also learned that construction but flow in an orderly fashion and inspection occurs in a specific order as well. I followed my plan and we tweaked things to adapt to any unforeseen changed that came our way and to the extent that was possible.

Here are some reasons why planning is important:

- Work out if you can achieve what you want.
- Think about how you are going to achieve what you want.
- Work out any extra support you might need.
- Work out if there are things in your life you would like more control over (new responsibilities).
- Think about what you might do if some things don't work out.
- Think about the changes you want to make.
- Plan to make these changes successfully.
- Be sure to write down your thoughts, as they are easy to forget.

For corporations, you remember when you started your organization you had to have a business plan. As time goes on, it is also important to plan to reexamine your initial business plan to make sure you are still on track with the plan. It is also important to have a business growth plan. Not reviewing your business plan and your business growth plan intermittently is a potential recipe for disaster.

One of the biggest challenges individuals and organizations face is the fact that plans for achieving a specific goal are typically clearly defined and mapped out; however they are not fully executed. In addition to this, one of the biggest mistakes most businesses and individuals make is that they fail to reexamine their original business plans and they fail to restructure them and tailor them to changing times and changing modalities within the businesses in themselves. Just like an individual needs a personal growth plan, every business also needs a business growth plan in order to remain successful and to keep up with the dynamics of the business itself.

COMMITMENT

He who would accomplish little need sacrifice little; he who would achieve much must sacrifice much. He who would attain highly must sacrifice greatly.
—James Allen, *As a Man Thinketh*

Merriam-Webster's Collegiate Dictionary defines commitment as a promise to do or give something: a promise to be loyal to someone or something: the attitude of someone who works very hard to do or support something.

Commitment simply means that you "walk the talk." It means you stick with it no matter what. It is a promise to finish what has been started.

When I first learned about the fable of the chicken and the pig a few months ago, it took me a long time to get it. I never heard it while growing up. I just could not get it. So I "Googled" it and read up more, then I got it! Of course, it is so true.

You want to be successful. You have to be committed. Again, success is simply a sense of accomplishment. A sense that you have achieved a positive and desired result. For example, you could be a great and caring mom or dad; that's a huge success. You could be a dedicated pastor, spouse, teacher, nurse, cook, business or owner, and a successful one too. To be successful in whatever your goal is takes commitment. You have to be committed. Just like in the fable of the chicken and the pig. To make the ham and eggs breakfast, the chicken simply laid the eggs, but the pig made the complete sacrifice for the breakfast—so the pig was committed.

As a leader in an organization, one has to be committed toward the mission and the goal of the organization. A leader has to believe in the ideas and ideals of the organization and should be capable of transforming them into real practices in the work field.

A committed leader will know how to promote the sense of commitment in his or her fellow team members so that they can work with the same zeal.

Here are some tips that helped me keep my team committed:

Stay positive.

Keep your employees' morale up and positive by giving positive reinforcement. Make your employees feel appreciated. People who are emotionally committed are more productive than those who are not.

Define expectations.

Each member of your team may be an expert at what they do, but you must clearly define what they need to do within your organization's framework. If you don't do this, they will lack direction. This leads to lack of productivity.

Address concerns.

When employee concerns are addressed, then of course their morale and commitment are reinforced. Always be available for questions, concerns, feedback, or to put the necessary systems in place for concerns to be addressed.

Open door policy.

Be open to innovative ideas and feedback from team members. Each employee should be aware of the fact that the leader is open to new ideas and that their suggestions will be taken into serious consideration and not stifled. Involve employees in barnstorming processes.

Stay connected.

A good leader should have a sense of connection with the team members even away from the corporation itself. It's always good for people away from work to still feel like a family so upon return to work the team spirit is maintained.

Foster Empowerment.

Employment opportunities that offer room for growth definitely improve employee satisfaction and thus their commitment. Training and development also help boost and improve employee motivation and thus their commitment.

Organizational commitment is a term used nowadays to describe the strength of an employee's emotional attachment to their place of employment. Understanding organizational commitment and applying its principles to your company can help the team stay emotionally attached to the company itself.

In 1991, Allen and Meyer described three components that influence how employees feel about the company they work for: affective, continuance, and normative. This was published in the *Human Resource Management Review*. These three components of employee commitment are thought to describe how people feel about their workplace, and this gives an idea of employee job satisfaction and hence the sense of well-being.

Normative commitment

This involves a sense of loyalty to the organization and causes employees to feel a sense of obligation to stay, whether they are happy or not. For example, a clinic was not doing too well financially, so much so that during extreme times, a few key employees did not receive a paycheck or the paycheck was delayed. The employees' loyalty kept them in the company without missing a beat. Normative commitment in employees is high where employees regularly see visible examples of the employer being committed to employee well-being. Normative commitment is great for employees to have but should not be misused by the employer.

Affective commitment

This is the emotional attachment of an employee to organizational values. The employee stays with the company because their goals line up with those of the organization's, and because of this, they choose to remain in employment.

When it comes to me personally and my medical profession, as well as helping others outside of the medical practice, I have affective commitment. I love helping people; that's my passion. So if I were to find myself in an environment that was not extremely favorable but I was able to add significant value to the people by improving their health or otherwise, I'll tend to stick with it. That's affective commitment.

Continuance commitment

Is a measure of the employees' dedication to staying with the company even if the conditions become less than ideal. For example, an employee has stayed in a company for a long time and they now worry about leaving for fear of loss of wages and benefits, loss of seniority, loss of coworker contacts, and so on and so forth. This form of commitment is common the longer people remain in employment at that company.

In order to maintain internal stability in a company, having experienced employees who are hard working is fantastic. However, this is not enough. It's also a huge plus if these employees stay with the company long term. When employees hang on long term, the company benefits from the employees' efforts and innovation.

So as a leader, if you understand these three components of employee commitment and actively strive to strike a balance between all three, you will in the long run increase your employee job satisfaction and thus decrease employee turnover.

Employee attrition and turnover are, in most cases, associated with increased cost to the company. From dampened morale leading to decreased productivity to administrative costs involved in the separation, employee turnover, especially if excessive, can lead to internal instability within the company itself.

In my clinic, for example, I have an employee who has been here from day one. She remains totally committed. Her performance and the value she brings to the company are priceless and unwavering. It is always good for companies to strive to keep good employees long term. The flip side of this is that companies need be careful about bad and toxic employees. A bad employee can be morally damaging to other employees. Employers should learn to quickly sever relationships between the company and the bad or toxic employee.

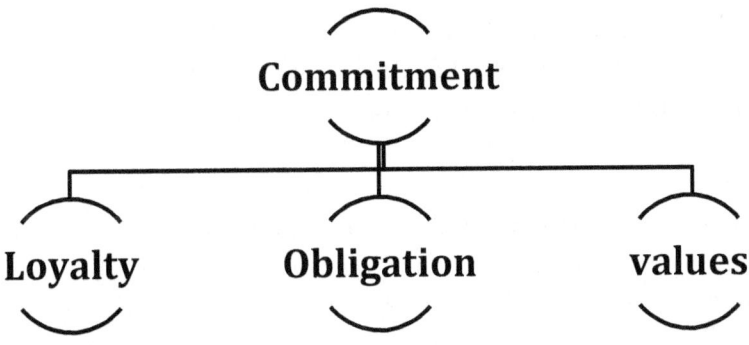

Commitment

Loyalty   **Obligation**   **values**

PERSONAL DEVELOPMENT

Personal development is the process of improving and growing one's awareness, skills, abilities, and thus, one's potential.

Personal development is so important, it can never be overstated. You have to develop yourself and grow, before you will ever be able to become the person that you want to become. Take time to do some soul searching. Start by thinking about where you are in life right now. Take time to reflect on the quality of your life. Are you happy about where you are right now? If you are happy and comfortable and want to stay where you are, then you will have a difficult time improving your environment. Improvement has to start with self.

Make a conscious effort to develop yourself. I'm not talking about skills for work. I'm talking about personal growth.

Don't get confused about personal development and personal improvement (which we will talk about later in this book). Personal development means adding new qualities to your life. Personal improvement means improving on the skills that you already have or on a specific area of your life.

According to John Maxwell, growth doesn't just happen. "Growth is essential to our satisfaction and our success, but it doesn't just happen." It means that you must take the time to study hard to develop yourself and to grow personally. It will not happen spontaneously. It happens only on purpose. You should have a plan for personal growth. No one ever grows by accident. John Maxwell goes on to say, "The greatest gap in the world in the gap between knowing and doing."

"People are anxious to improve their circumstances but are unwilling to improve themselves. They therefore remain bound."
—James Allen

It's time to start thinking about what areas of your life you would like to develop.

James Allen, in his book *As a Man Thinketh,* says, "Every man is where he is by the law of his being; the thoughts which he has built into his character have brought him there, and in the arrangement of his life there is no element of chance, but all is the result of a law which cannot err. This is just as true of those who feel 'out of harmony' with their surroundings as of those who are contented with them."

A very wise man, James Allen (1864–1912), a very powerful motivational writer, sums up that a person's character is the sum of all his thoughts.

I would like you to be very mindful of three things that are important for personal development.

a) Your thoughts. Positive thinking will fertilize the internal environment within you for personal development. Negative thinking will clutter your mind. I look at negative thinking like a bunch of weeds growing together with a bed of roses. Remove those weeds, and you will note that the flowers do so much better.

b) Your relationships. Most of our relationships are social ones. For example, we have our family, friends, coworkers, and mentors. Some of these are nourishing, and that's great. They help you to grow and reach your greatest potential. Others are toxic. Knowingly or unintentionally, these kinds of relationships are full of negativity. They bring you down and can potentially create turmoil that stunts your own personal development. Make every effort to distance yourself from toxic relationships.

c) Your network. Make an effort to improve your professional relationships by simply networking with and collaborating with other like-minded people. If you are in marketing, get in contact with and network with other marketers. If you are a professional, attend some conferences in your field. If you are a stay-at-home mom, meet up with some moms and see what everybody is doing. You'll learn so much more from like-minded people than from remaining alone inside your own niche.

In order to reach your fullest potential as individuals as well as a member of a team or even as an employee in a company, a specific plan for professional and personal growth is part of your responsibility. You must strive to grow your potential within your scope of employment in order for you to elevate your position within the company. Some companies have personal development programs.

For the past five to six years, I had been invited to churches, conferences, and events to speak. At a certain point, I made a decisions to become a professional speaker. Not long after I made this decision, I decided to increase my personal development. I found out that John C Maxwell, one of the greatest experts on leadership, had an online training group. Of course, I immediately joined.

When I first signed up to become a member of the John Maxwell's group, I was so excited about the extensive nature of the fantastically valuable information that was available to me. Within a short space of time, I realized that I was very interested in everything. I mean every single link I opened, I said to myself, "I need that." Keeping in mind that John Maxwell is author of over seventy books, as well as five extensive learning systems, you can imagine how much information I had available to me; it could take me years to study everything. The overachiever in me immediately kicked in. I started to study as much as I could and went from one learning system to the other without any specific structure or plan. Within two months of reading through and not mastering anything, I realized it was important for me to put some structure or a plan to my study. So I joined the John Maxwell Ninety Days to Success road map designed by the John Maxwell group, and this allowed me to study the John Maxwell philosophy and teaching in a structured and effective manner so I could add value to other people's lives.

I say these just to give you an idea of the fact that any study or knowledge acquisition should be done in a structured manner for it to be effective. Remember that as you create a personal growth plan, one of the areas to leverage is your own life experience. Leveraging your own personal past experiences will help guide and personalize your plan for growth.

Personal growth can impact your relationships at work and with your family. Here's a list of my personal top nine areas for personal growth and development. You should think and make up your own list and work on adding one personal growth factor at a time. Keep each factor developing as you slowly add and/or master the others.

- faith
- health
- financial
- relationships
- goal setting
- planning
- character
- time management
- communication

As you see, personal development is a journey. But then again, life's a journey.

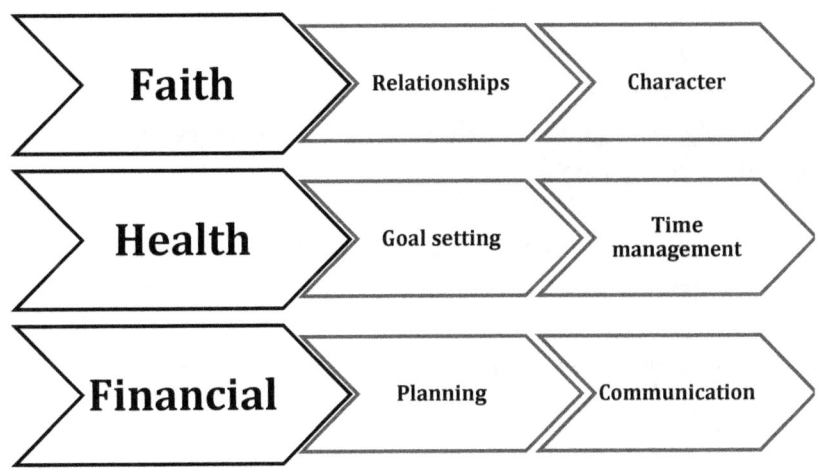

GOAL DRIVEN

Imagine an end point or a desired result. Imagine yourself striving continuously to get to that end point or result. That's the meaning of goal driven. Setting goals is a very fundamental compliment for achieving long-term success.

A simple way of looking at this is that you cannot get to where you're trying to go until you clearly define where it is that you are going. Setting goals helps everyone, whether individuals or employees in an organization or children in school. It helps everyone be aware of what is expected as the outcome of a specific objective. Also achieving a specific goal gives individuals the feeling of success, and this in turn generates increased desire to achieve more.

There are several reasons why it is important to set individual goals. Having a goal motivates you and keeps you focused when your attention starts to wax and wane. Goals give us this zeal and help fuel the determination to keep moving forward. Goals help us believe in ourselves and give us the opportunity to evaluate failure.

The leader needs to be goal driven. They need to be the one to motivate the whole team to work together toward achievement of a specific goal.

Now back to you. How do you become or improve on the goal-driven qualities of your personality?

This is the time to challenge yourself. Maintaining focus and in becoming engaged in the process to achieve that goal will keep you goal oriented. In so doing, you can become world class at whatever it is that you are focusing on. Strive to see the end in your mind.

The following strategies helped to keep me focused on a goal:

1. Set clear goals.
2. Make a specific plan.
3. Set timelines.
4. Prioritize.
5. Stay focused.
6. Track progress.
7. Celebrate goal achievement.

One of my personal goals since January 2010 has been to keep my cholesterol under good control through diet and exercise. After four years of doing this, I have realized that for my workout to be effective and for me to remain focused during my workout, I should have a specific goal in mind before I get to the gym. For example, complete five miles in an hour plus free weights (upper body, four muscle groups), three sets in twenty minutes. This type of plan keeps me focused and helps me complete a meaningful and effective workout.

Similar principles hold for keeping a company goal driven. In an organization, it's up to the leader to have strategies in place for keeping the team focused on achieving the goal thus the success of the company itself.

The steps for keeping everyone in a company engaged and focused on the goal are similar.

- Define clear goals in line with the mission of the company.
- Establish the process to achieve the goals.
- Set realistic timelines.
- Review performance regularly.

- Manage and measure accountability.
- Monitor progress.
- Determine Rewards/bonuses.

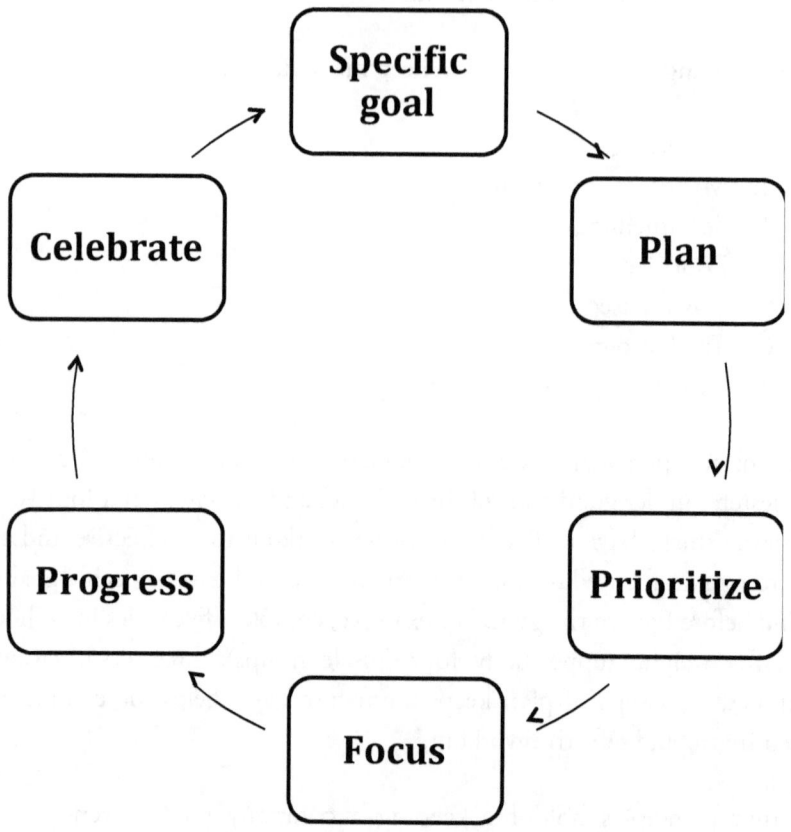

FOCUS

Staying focused is one of the key elements to success. The lack of focus and the multitude of distractions we have within and around us will limit your ability to achieve success. Think about this: it is impossible to focus on two things at a time. So you must become very selective on what you allow your mind to stay focused on. Maintaining focus is one of the key disciplines that will allow you to achieve success.

Everyone who works in the clinic knows that I remain focused while I am seeing patients. If you walk up to me and say something, I may hear you, but it will not register. Unless it is an emergency, then I allow myself to shift focus. It's a habit that I have trained myself in, and it has allowed me to accomplish a lot.

Most of the time, before I set out on a task, I typically set a time in which I will do nothing but focus on that task. I usually set no more than an hour. I sit and don't get up, don't answer my phone, and don't text. Nothing but the task at hand. When the hour is up, I allow my focus to shift. If I am not done, I usually take a zero- to fifteen-minute break and come back to the task. It just depends on what I am doing. Try this routine.

A leader's ability to focus brings forth the aspects of creativity and innovation within the organization. There are so many things around us which cause distraction so before we proceed. Let us together examine a few things that may be distracting and interrupting our focus.

o   social media
o   mobile phones/text messages

o television/loud music
o intrusive thoughts
o poor or lack of planning
o lack of clear goals and expectations
o lack of proper skills

Let us examine a few things that we can do to help us stay on track and get us closer to achieving our goals

1. **Plan.** Every evening, plan your day ahead. Make a list of all tasks and items you must complete the following day. Prioritize your list and complete important items first.

2. **Focus your mind on one single task at a time**. Develop this skill and ability to direct your mind fully to one task at a time. Master the art of mental focus by taking control over your mind and being aware of what your mind is focusing on.

3. Develop a habit of **narrowing your focus** with determined intensity on one key item at a time. Keep your attention zeroed in on only one single task for at least sixty to ninety minutes each time. Taking a five- to ten-minute break every sixty minutes will improve your performance.

4. **Eliminate distraction from the environment.** Don't allow intrusive distractions, such as text messages, pages, and phone calls, to interrupt your focus. So in order to stay focused, you must find and make a habit of shutting down these distractions that may be intruding into your focus or slowing down or limiting your productivity.

5. **Eliminate intrusive thoughts.** Avoid the habit of allowing your mind to travel around while you are focusing on a different task. When you learn how to focus, your mind you will also learn how to use it effectively to complete the tasks that you have on hand.

The human mind has the capacity to focus only on one item at a time. You can practice this exercise on your own. It is impossible to think of two separate tasks at the same time. In order to think of two things at a time, you will have to stop thinking of one of them and then let your mind travel to the other. By this same token, to learn how to remain focused, you must train your mind stay focused on one task at a time's until that task is completed.

I must mention that in order to stay focused, you must improve and maintain your internal environment as well. Therefore, a healthy lifestyle is crucial. Avoid mind-altering substances like prescription narcotic medications, alcohol, and illicit drugs, and develop healthy habits, such as proper nutrition, adequate hydration with water, and regular exercise.

If you are reading this book and admit that you are addicted to any mind-altering substances, I urge you to seek immediate help. Your health is paramount to success.

MIND-SET DEVELOPMENT

Cherish your visions. Cherish your ideals.

*Cherish the music that stirs in your heart, the beauty that forms
in your mind, the loveliness that drapes your purest thoughts.*

*For out of them will grow all delightful conditions,
all heavenly environment, of these, if you but remain
true to them, your world will at last be built.*

—James Allen, *As a Man Thinketh*

The mind-set can be defined as the established set of attitudes held by someone. It is also simply defined as a person's way of thinking. It is a set of assumptions or notations held by one more people or groups of people that is so established that it creates a powerful incentive within these people or groups to continue to adopt or accept certain behaviors or choices. A mind-set can also be seen as a person's philosophy of life.

Mind-set development is such an important aspect of personal growth and development that it cannot be overstated.

Our mind-sets determine how we think and how we interact with everyone around us. They govern our decisions and determine our judgments and our own personal criticism that we have unconsciously created within ourselves. So having a positive mind-set is important for personal sustainability. A negative mind-set or a fixed mind-set can prevent us from achieving our goals and our destiny.

Positivity is the inside job that makes the world around you look better. Remember that you cannot control life. You cannot control people. You cannot sit and wait and hope for the world around you to change, but you control how you react to life.

Research shows that positive thinking, positive attitude, and optimism may improve your overall health.

Some of the health benefits of positive thinking may include

- increased life span
- lower rates of depression
- greater resistance to common colds
- lower risk of death from heart disease
- better psychological and physical well-being
- better coping skills during hard times

Remember the powerful concept that it's not about what happens to us; it's how we react to what happens to us. It's important not to allow failures or trials to interrupt our momentum. It's important to stay motivated, stay to cause, and keep a positive attitude.

So it is clear that positive thinking and a positive attitude will create positive results. It will make things easier.

So let us look at ten steps that helped me develop a positive mind-set.

1. **Take charge of yourself.** Believing that you are responsible for yourself and your life is crucial for mind-set development. You are responsible. Don't allow anyone to take charge of your life.

2. **Laugh.** We all remember the old saying "Laughter is the best medicine." It really is! Keep a good sense of humor as often as

possible. It will certainly contribute to your happiness. Remember that *you* can make *you* happy!

3. **Think positive.** Commit yourself to always thinking in positive ways. Feel your mind with positive things. Don't dwell on negativity. Remember the concept of the half-full or the half-empty glass? This simple concept explains how an optimistic perception is unique to everyone's simple interpretation of reality.

4. **Input.** Control and reduce the amount of negative input that you receive. The world around us feeds us with a lot of negativity. From the TV stations to the Internet, friends, family, and colleagues, we are constantly bombarded with negative information. Make every effort to stay clear of these kinds of input. They can have a negative impact on our mind-sets.

5. **Gratitude.** Be grateful every day for everything that you have. Being thankful for yourself or your life, for your relationships, and for the your situation in life is critical to helping you appreciate the abundance that you have.

6. **Health.** Taking care of your body will enable you to have a positive mind. Exercise is known to release happy hormones that will help give us a positive mind-set. Avoid ingesting toxins that can affect your thought process, like drugs and alcohol.

7. **Less worry.** Make every effort not to dwell on negative things that happened to you. As we have said, you cannot control life. But you can control how you react to life. Worrying and dwelling on things that you cannot control will do nothing but create a negative mind-set.

8. **Relationships.** Take inventory of your relationships. Stick with those that elevate you to the next levels. Turn away from people who lack the capacity to see value in you. Distance yourself from people who consistently try to bring you down.

9. **Smile.** Smiling has been shown to keep you happy, even when you are down and out. Also, smiling gives other people a good impression about you. Remember people's expressions as you tend to mirror your expressions at them.

10. **Life.** Embrace life the way it is. Focus your mind on things that are important to you. Love yourself and live life fully with everything that you have right now.

It is imperative to control your reactions to events around you. Keep in mind that life is a journey and it is important that we live it.

Realize that it's not about what happens to you; it's how you react to what happens in life. "Life" happens to everyone! But not everyone is down and out because of unfavorable life circumstances. You cannot control life, but you control how you react to it.

COURAGE

Courage is defined as the ability to do something that frightens one. From ancient times to modern day, from children's fairy tales and movies to reports of acts of bravery, courage has been exemplified as a positive character and one of respect. In the same light, courage and bravery are good attributes for corporate leaders and people in general to possess in order to be successful.

Ralph Waldo Emerson said, "Whatever you do, you need courage. Whatever course you decide upon, there is always someone to tell you that you are wrong. There are always difficulties arising that temp you to believe your critics are right. To map out a course of action and follow it to an end requires some of the same courage that a soldier needs."

Leadership takes courage. No matter where you are in life, whether it is at home, in a business, in a relationship, as a teacher, as a student, as a homemaker, or as a religious personality, it doesn't really matter. Courage is a crucial attribute to possess in order to be successful. Contrary to what most people believe, courage is a skill that can be learned and acquired.

Growing up as a young girl, I was very shy and timid. However, going through and coming out of "the fire of life" trials and tribulations have helped me learn this critical virtue that I need for continued success.

The benefits of courage in the workplace are many. We know several successful interpreters like Steve Jobs and Walt Disney possessed tremendous courage and were able to build very successful industries. Some of the benefits of courage in the workplace include increased innovation, great brand recognition, higher customer service, high employee engagement, increased innovation, and successful marketing.

Seven Steps That Helped Me Develop Courage

1. **Dream big.** The courage to dream and set goals can be challenging, but it is worthwhile and will help you develop courage.

2. **Step out of your comfort zone.** The courage of stretching one's self a little into a brand-new zones which we have never explored, will give us new confidence and hence the courage to reach new heights.

3. **Face your fears.** Running away consistently from situations that cause stress and anxiety that we must deal with is the worst outcome possible. So we must resolve to accept negative outcomes and take action to correct these.

4. **Take responsibility for your actions and results.** Being committed to achieving your goals and your dreams also comes with the responsibility of becoming faced with any outcome. Facing this reality will help you develop courage.

5. **Be ready to make mistakes.** Remember that in everything you do, you must realize that you will make a mistake, but be ready to learn from their mistakes and have the courage to understand that if you make a mistake, it is simply that mistake. Learn from it and move on.

6. **Be independent.** Learning to stand on your own and facing new challenges will help you develop courage. Repeatedly leaning on others or looking to others for support in every decision that you make will limit or reduce your ability to become courageous.

7. **Be confident.** Be comfortable and confident with the choices that you make. Have faith in yourself. Teach yourself as well as those around you the benefit of self-confidence and perseverance because most of the time the outcome is courage.

CONSISTENCY

For every choice that you make, for every goal and dream, for every plan that you have, you must be consistent over time in order to be successful.

Your life today is a result of all the choices that you have made over time. So you must take responsibility to examine these choices and make them constructive; otherwise, wrong choices, repeated over time, will lead to disaster.

As the owner and CEO of a medical facility, I personally review every single progress note and test result for all patients that are seen in the clinic before the chart can be finalized and the clinic can be reimbursed for that patient contact visit.

It is obvious to me that should I fall behind on my work, it will have a negative impact of clinic finances. So I have learned to pace myself when I seem to be pulled in different directions. I make a specific effort to time myself for at least one hour with no interruptions to complete my work in order to prevent negative financial impact and consequences on the facility itself. So you see how if I fall behind on my work, or lack consistency, the clinic is impacted negatively. The consistency in what I do will show for the clinic success. And at the times that I have to be away from the clinic, I keep this duty consistent by involving other licensed physicians to complete this task so the task is a consistent one, regardless of my ability to personally do it.

It is the consistency in the actions in all the things that we do in life that make a positive impact. You must be consistent in your personal habits and in your professional behavior in order to succeed. Doing it once won't cut it. You have to do it over and over.

Another example is a weight-loss program. I have had a life long struggle with my weight. I finally realized, of course, my problem was lack of consistency with time. Most people who are overweight can agree with me on this one. I will start a diet, lose the weight, and then stop doing whatever I was doing to keep the weight off and gain the weight back—and more. Let us look at an example closely. If you simply cut out two hundred to three hundred calories per day from your diet, that means giving up the french fries and that extra milk shake and eating baked chicken instead of fried chicken. You figure out what small sacrifice you will be able to make over time. So let's do the math. Getting read of 3,500 calories will mean you lose one pound. This means you will lose two to three pounds in a month. And in a year, you will lose about twenty to thirty pounds. So you see how a small sacrifice over time adds up. Let's look at another example.

Most people have heard the concept of the Magic Penny Doubling Effect. If you were given the choice between taking four million dollars in cash today or a single penny that doubles in value every day for thirty-one days, which would you choose?

Most people would choose the four million dollars, right? I would say one penny, and here's the reason why. On day five, I would have sixteen cents. By day twenty, my one penny is now five thousand dollars. On day twenty-eight, that penny is now over one million dollars. On day thirty-one, the penny is now just over ten million dollars. Now you see the extreme reward you can receive by making small, smart choices over time.

Let's look at a visual.

Choose **$3 million in cash** today or a **single penny** that doubles in value every day for 31 days, which would you choose?

	You	Your Friend
Day 1	$3,000,0000	$0.01
Day 5	$3,000,0000	$0.16
Day 10	$3,000,0000	$5.00
Day 20	$3,000,0000	$5,000
Day 28	$3,000,0000	$1,342,177.28
Day 31	$3,000,0000	$10,737,418.24

So in summary, consistency is crucial to success. Whether it is in the relationship with your spouse, with your significant other, with your children, with your coworkers, with your employees, or with you spirituality leaders, it is important to continue doing and improving the things that created a positive outcome.

Tips that helped me stay consistent.

1. Do it.

2. Do it even when the going gets tough.

3. Do it even when you are tired.

4. Do it regardless.

5. Do it every day.

SECTION 2: PRODUCTIVITY

Productivity

Productivity is simply the ability to get the job done!

PLANNING

After several years in the work force, one cannot help but be curious about how successful people stay productive. Some people have a lot on their plates but consistently get things done! Others (and this happens to many of us) seem to spend the whole workday being pulled left and right, being extremely busy but not quite accomplishing the key tasks or projects that they hoped to have put the final "full stop" on!

Why is it that some high achievers have full plates but accomplish things in a timely manner anyway? What are the specific key functions that they perform that make them seemingly come out ahead of the rest of us more often than not?

Let's start by looking at what some of the most successful people of our times do to stay productive. I found this article at INC.com about "10 Leaders and the Surprising Ways They Stay Productive" (http://www.inc.com/ss/10-leaders-and-the-surprising-ways-they-stay-productive?slide=1#2). Here are the two leaders that struck me the most.

Stephen King advocates *consistency* as one of the key attributes to success. In his 2000 autobiography *On Writing,* he advises to writers who want to be successful to write every day. Writing every day, including Saturdays and Sundays, is how Stephen King was able to write forty-five novels that have sold millions of copies.

Arianna Huffington, Internet publishing pioneer, advocates for *sleep* She is the president and editor-in-chief of the Huffington Post Media Group. Her web universe attracts 250 million unique visitors each month. She states, "My single most effective trick for getting things done is to stop doing what I'm doing and get some sleep."

The late Steve Jobs, who was the cofounder, chairman, and CEO of Apple, had his executive team focus intensely on three to four projects over a period of time—and if your project was outside their realm, you were out of luck. One of the things that jumps out at me from the extensive Steve Jobs biography (http://allaboutstevejobs.com) was that he maintained radical focus on what he was best at: creating products, recruiting, marketing, and of course, being the public face of the company. He described it in a 2004 interview. "I get to spend my time on the forward-looking stuff. My top executives take half the other work off my plate. They love it, and I love it."

Oprah Winfrey's success is simply based on her belief that you become what you believe. Her unwavering belief in her abilities is what drove her to focus all of her energy on reaching her objectives. Once successful on one objective, she will then allow herself to move to the next. Her single-minded focus allowed her to concentrate all of her time and energy into achieving the life of her dreams. Oprah's net worth at the time I wrote this book stands at $2.9 billion dollars.

Here's a list of thirty things I did to improve my productivity.

1. Focus on what is important.
2. Start working as soon as you get to work.
3. Wake up early.
4. Exercise three to five times a week.
5. Make a list of five distractions and work toward eliminating them.
6. Limit or schedule your social media tasking.
7. Get enough sleep.
8. Spend time with family and friends.
9. Schedule date nights with your spouse or partner.
10. Avoid procrastination.

11. Watch less TV. It's actually better to stop watching TV.
12. Don't skip breakfast.
13. Make a list of things you need to stop doing.
14. Eliminate multitasking.
15. Prioritize your work.
16. Set goals for yourself: immediate, short-term, and long-term goals.
17. Plan your day ahead and write it down.
18. De-clutter your mind.
19. Learn to say no.
20. Follow doctors' orders.
21. Stay positive.
22. Think before you act.
23. Smile and laugh often.
24. Celebrate achievements.
25. Generate an emergency fund.
26. Don't argue with others.
27. Give to charity.
28. Take charge of your life. Don't let anyone be in charge of you.
29. Start a hobby.
30. Be accountable to yourself.

When it comes to productivity in a corporation, it is important to stay practical, analytical, and have clearly defined and implemented strategies for measuring productivity.

Every business and organization should have strategies integrated into the business model for measuring productivity. For over twenty years, documented productivity planning strategies have assisted many companies, managers, sales professionals, and leaders to develop their skills and improve their companies' performance.

These must be integrated in the business model. Keeping things as simple and as straightforward and practical as possible is important.

In the business life, a productivity plan should address all areas that may potentially affect the overall productivity of the individual or the association.

Every company or organization should have a set of policies and procedures for achieving the company's objectives. In organizations, there are three main types of planning used in management. These are strategic planning, tactical planning, and operational planning.

a. **Strategic planning** must be in line with the business goals and mission.

This deals with the long-term goals of the company. For most companies, *long-term* means three to five years, whereas for others, it means ten to twenty years. This involves the foundation and analysis of the business vision and mission as well as the core value of the raison d'être of the company itself. So this keeps in mind what specific outcome is expected because of the company's operations and how these operations are fulfilled. It is important, while outlining a strategic plan, to complete an external analysis of factors beyond the control of the company itself. In other words, the strategic plan is designed to align day-to-day work activities with the overall mission of the organization. Then in order for the strategic plan to be effective, it has to be analyzed against the external forces of the company. For example, performing a SWOT analysis will identify the business strengths, weaknesses, opportunities, and threats. Several other tools can be used for strategic planning.

b. **Tactical planning,** on the other hand, deals which short-term goals and specific actions necessary to achieve those goals and objectives outlined in the strategic plan. For most companies, *short-term* means less than a year. Tactical planning needs to articulate who is responsible for achieving the specific objectives of each of the tasks outlined this strategic plan itself. The tactical plans are typically developed in the areas of personnel, marketing, and finance. Tactical plans are usually developed by the lower-level managers who are intricately and directly involved in the day-to-day operations of the company.

c. **Operational planning** deals with the direct day-to-day functioning of the company itself. Operational planning determines all the goals outlined in that tactical plan of the company. For example, in our medical clinic, the operational plan of the front desk determines how the patients are received when they arrive at the clinic until they are received by the nurse.

We must keep in mind that strategic plans, tactical plans, and operational plans of every company are intertwined with one another and together they aid in the achievement of the overall company's goals. These plans must be examined often and modified in order to keep the company productive.

It is also a good idea to have a contingency plan in place. This gives the company something to fall back on in case the original plan fails.

What about personal productivity? How do you make sure you finish a project that you started? Are you familiar with working hard but not quite completing the task or not quite achieving the anticipated result? If you are not productive in your personal life, then here are a few tips you can build into your life, two or three at a time. These may help you *Grow to Success* in your personal life and enable you to get the things that matter to you done. So go ahead and jumpstart your productivity with these tips.

PROBLEM SOLVING

Here are three definitions of problem solving that I found.

The term *problem solving* is used in many disciplines, sometimes with different perspectives and often with different terminologies.

For instance, it is a mental process in psychology and a computerized process in computer science. Problems can also be classified into two different types (ill-defined and well-defined) from which appropriate solutions are to be made. Ill-defined problems are those that do not have clear goals or solution paths, while well-defined problems have specific goals and clearly defined solution paths *(Wikipedia)*.

The process of working through details of a problem to reach a solution. Problem solving may include mathematical or systematic corporations and can be a gauge of an individual's critical thinking skills (BuisinessDictionary.com).

Process involved in finding a solution to a problem. Many animals routinely solve problems of accommodation, food finding, and shelter simply through trial and error. Some higher animals, such as apes, have demonstrated more complex problem-solving abilities, including discrimination of abstract stimuli, rule learning, and application of language or language-like operations. Humans use not only trial and error but also insight based on an understanding of principles, inductive and deductive reasoning (see deduction, induction, and logic), and divergent or creative thinking (see creativity). Problem-solving abilities and styles may vary considerably by individual (Merriam-Webster.com).

I like this definition: the process of working through details of a problem to reach a solution.

A simple and straightforward way of looking at problem solving is to figure out how to come up with a solution once you have a problem at hand.

John C. Maxwell, the international leadership expert, describes problem solving, especially when it involves teamwork, as fitting the right person in the right place at the right time.

> *"The Wrong Person in the Wrong Place = Regression. The Wrong Person in the Right Place = Frustration. The Right Person in the Wrong Place = Confusion. The Right Person in the Right Place = Progression. The Right People in the Right Places = Multiplication."*
> —John Maxwell.

Let us examine the simple basic steps in effective problem solving. As the CEO of American Stat Care Centers, I am used to problems surfacing at all levels. Anything from patient management to inventory and supply ordering and personnel management—problems in any entity are the norm. One must follow simple steps to thoroughly address the problems.

1. Identify the problem.

    One day, a patient came into the office with dehydration. It was obvious this patient needed to receive some rehydration intravenously. This meant we needed to insert a small catheter into her arm and simply administer a bag of fluids over one to two hours, since she was too ill to drink the fluids. The nurse went in search of the equipment needed and could not find a catheter. I was in shock. We are a very busy clinic. Inventory and ordering of supplies should be done on a weekly basis. These catheters are used infrequently, so I would assume we should never run out of these.

2. Identify the cause or causes of the problem.

    This means that you analyze the problem. In the case of the patient above, we could not find a catheter anywhere. Asking questions from one nurse to the other in the middle of a very busy day was not going to solve the problem. I quickly figured out that I needed to look into the procedure used for ordering supplies. I mean we use at least thirty-five to forty different supplies in the clinic. How can one person remember what is missing if it is completely out of stock? There is a supply checklist with all supplies listed. So what is the problem? Is this item missing from the checklist or is the person using the checklist not thorough enough?

3. Come up with solutions. Involve the team.

    When there's a problem, it's always good to involve the team. They may have better ideas than you have. Involving the team shows that you care about their in put.

    After the above incident, I had discussions with the nursing staff, and then we came up with a solution that seemed to resolve the issue for now. The supply order list had been checked by one of the nurses who worked in the clinic so infrequently that the catheters had never been used during her shift so she simply overlooked them. Well, now her awareness has been raised. She now knows we need these catheters and she must check that.

4. Develop a plan.

    Back to our example above, not only is the inventory list done by one nurse, it is crosschecked by a second nurse. This way, nothing is missed.

5. Implement the plan.

    In our example above, the plan was implemented right away.

6. Monitor the progress.

    The progress of our inventory and supply ordering will be monitored on a weekly basis.

    Look at a visual concept of the problem solving protocol.

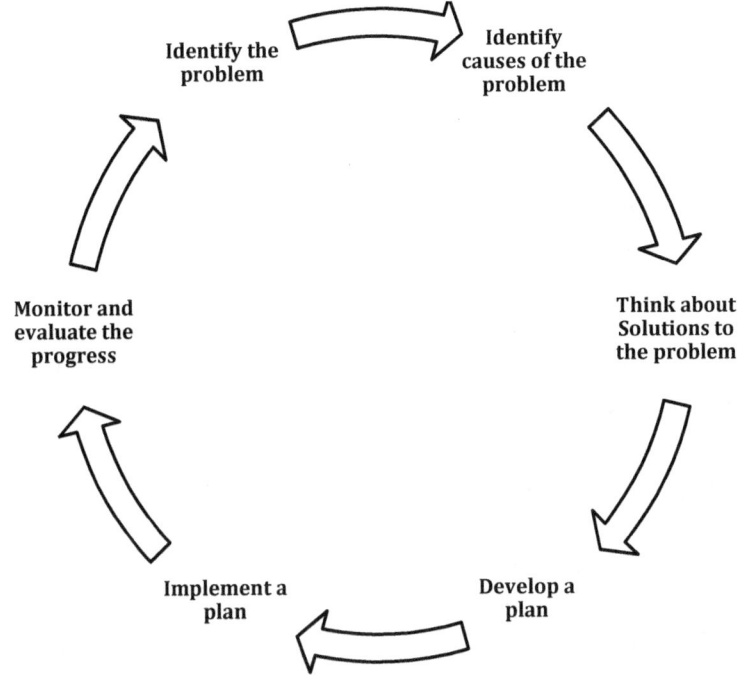

TIME MANAGEMENT

Time management is the act or process of planning and exercising conscious control over the amount of time spent on specific activities, especially to increase effectiveness, efficiency, or productivity (*Wikipedia*).

Have you ever gone home thinking how busy your day has been, how you have been overwhelmed with a lot of tasks but at the same time been unable to complete your day's work? Do you ever feel like you need twenty-five-hour days? Many of us know how it feels to get to work and then things come from every direction. You are responsible for multiple operations at the office. Your workday is interrupted by phone calls, questions from other colleagues and coworkers, and more. At the end of the day, it seems like tasks you should have completed are not done. All you had was a long, busy, frustrating day. You were busy all right, but not much was accomplished. So you return to work the next day already behind. Sometimes, we just have too many bad habits that break our focus, such as texting or keeping up with the social media updates of Facebook, LinkedIn, and others while at work.

According to the Mayo Clinic, managing your time effectively will help you not only get more done each day, but it has important health benefits too. By managing your time more wisely, you can minimize stress and improve your quality of life. Effective time management leads to improved productivity, which leads to success, less stress, and improved quality of life at work and away from work.

Now is the time to stop and think about how you spend your time every day. Are your tasks completed daily? Effective time management is the ability to plan and control how you spend the hours in your day to be able to accomplish your goals. Poor time management can be related to poor organizational skills, procrastination, lack of self-control, and the inability to pace ourselves or set boundaries for ourselves.

Time is such a fleeting commodity! It is one of those precious things that fly by, cannot be recuperated, and can be one of the major stress factors that managers face today. Everyone in the workforce has to deal with deadlines and other time constraints on a daily basis. Ever felt like there is too much to do in a day and not enough time to do it? Ever heard of the saying "Time is money"? Is it, or is it not?

Learn to focus your mind effectively and learn the foundation of time-management and productivity. Think about your self-worth and make every effort to stop doing the things that would cost you less than what it takes you to do it. For example, don't spend four hours buying supplies and fixing the broken fence when you can pay someone a lot less than what it took you to do it yourself. Remember the 80/20 principle: 20 percent of customers equal 80 percent of sales? This principle also applies to time management.

Here are some skills to help you manage your time more effectively:

1. You must know your goals.
2. Plan your day ahead—every day. Write it down.
3. Establish priorities.
4. Tackle tough and important jobs first.
5. Schedule "block times" of thirty to sixty minutes when you are not to be interrupted so you can work on a major task.
6. Divide large tasks into smaller ones and then tackle them one at a time until they are all done.
7. Delegate to others tasks that you are not expert in.
8. Hire a personal assistant.
9. List similar tasks together so they are completed at the same time.

10. Use idle time wisely, for example to clean and organize your desk and to plan for the next day.
11. De-clutter your desk.
12. Don't be a perfectionist.
13. Avoid procrastinating.
14. Limit the number of meetings you have every day.
15. Learn to say no to tasks that are not related to your goals.
16. Learn to say no to yourself.
17. Minimize socializing at work.
18. Avoid micro-management.
19. Take a break when you need to. Rest so that you are not exhausted and emotionally drained.
20. Improve your efficiency with a healthy lifestyle. Eat healthy, and exercise regularly.

COMMITMENT

*Above all be of single aim; have a legitimate and useful
purpose, and devote yourself unreservedly to it.*
—James Allen

Merriam-Webster's Collegiate Dictionary defines commitment as a promise
to do or give something; a promise to be loyal to someone or something;
the attitude of someone who works very hard to do or support something.

I love the fable about the ham and egg breakfast. "The chicken was involved,
but the pig was committed." In order to make this breakfast, the chicken
simply lays the egg. But the pig had to sacrifice everything to make the
ham. With this fable in mind, you must be completely committed to your
goals in order to accomplish them.

As president and CEO of American Stat Care Clinic, I have been involved
in recruiting many employees. In this small city, West Monroe, everybody
knows almost everybody. And almost everyone knows about the clinic.
So most job seekers are quite familiar with the clinic at the time of their
interview. I can just tell in my gut who is enthusiastic about the position and
who is not. Over time, I note that those who were most enthusiastic in the
beginning are those who remain committed to the mission of the clinic itself.

If you are the leader of a corporation, you must display a significant level
of commitment, and then all those who work for you will simply sense
your level of commitment and mirror it. Uncommitted leaders are one of
the major reasons for failure of even the most promising establishments.

Commitment simply means that you "walk the talk." It means you stay with it no matter what. It is a promise to finish what has been started. As a leader in an organization, one has to be committed to the mission and the goal of the organization. A leader has to believe in the ideas and ideals of the organization and should be capable of transforming them into real practices in the work field.

A committed leader will know how to promote the sense of commitment in her or his fellow team members so that they can work with the same zeal as her or him.

Commitment, in all that you do, in all that you put your heart into, will help every business, relationship, friendship, and partnership thrive and reach greater heights. Commitment to unity in marriage is one of the key factors that can keep a difficult institution like marriage thriving, regardless of the odds.

Lack of personal motivation can lead to a decline in commitment on the job. This is never good. Don't allow your personal lack of motivation and decreased interest or drive affect your company's productivity. The same goes for your personal life and relationships especially in an important relationship like marriage, where lack of motivation can threaten one's commitment. And this threatens the marriage itself. Take action now. Evaluate your commitment and improve on it often.

Tips that helped me stay committed to my passion:

1. Develop clear goals.
2. Plan. Develop a roadmap to accomplish your goals.
3. Model commitment to your goals.
4. Record your thoughts in a journal.
5. Track your progress.
6. Think about your results.
7. Give your employees challenging responsibilities incrementally.
8. Keep a journal of your progress.
9. Invest time and money wisely.
10. Review your work regularly.

GROWTH AND DEVELOPMENT

The *Wikipedia* online dictionary defines personal growth and development as "activities that improve awareness and identity, develop talents and potential, build human capital and facilitate employability, enhance quality of life and contribute to the realization of dreams and aspirations." When personal development takes place in the context of institutions, it refers to the methods, programs, tools, techniques, and assessment systems that support human development at the individual level in organizations.

You are your greatest asset, so why not improve your own value by improving yourself?

Investing your resources in your own personal development is one of the smartest and most worthwhile investments you can make. It will add value to your life and amplify your potential for lasting success and personal fulfillment.

Adding value to individuals inevitably trickles down to the company. It is important to build a strong mind-set, discover your purpose in life, and learn to tap into your passion. Build a powerful vision and learn to set goals, and take action on them.

Why is there so much emphasis nowadays on personal growth and development? Let me spell it out for you. You will never be able to do better than yourself. So you must improve on and develop yourself in order to elevate yourself to the next level. First, you must take the time to think about yourself and about what areas you want to improve in yourself. Determine what your end results should be. You have to become aware of the need to change and then actively work on it. You must develop yourself in order to improve on yourself and your surroundings. Your mind is the most powerful organ in your body, so developing your mind and yourself is critical for growth. If you will change, your circumstances will change.

Working actively on your personal growth and development will empower you and literally set you on a personal transformational process, which will improve your physical, emotional, intellectual, spiritual, professional, and financial situation.

> *"Confront your inadequacies and push your personal boundaries: It's the surest way to grow, improve, and expand the scope of your influence."*
> —John C. Maxwell

Areas of growth and development that helped me *Grow to Success.*

1. Faith
2. Finances
3. Character
4. Relationships
5. Career
6. Health
7. Attitude
8. Personality
9. Communication
10. Learning
11. Goal setting
12. Time management

For business owners, developing a business growth strategy provides an opportunity to ensure improved profitability, greater clarity and more confidence on plans, an exit plan if needed, and managed growth over time.

Business development typically focuses on one or more of the following areas, depending on the company's needs:

- planning new services
- marketing and promoting
- financial forecasting
- developing a business growth strategy
- utilizing customer feedback
- ongoing education

MARKETING

The American Marketing Association defines marketing as the activity, set of institutions, and processes for creating, communicating, delivering, and exchanging offerings that have value for customers, clients, partners, and society at large.

Read the definition closely and underline the fact that your product should add value to the customer. In other words, your service or product should satisfy customers while making profits.

Also, you must consider your competition. What are the things you have to think about in order to position yourself against the competition? Your customer wants to know why they should buy from you as opposed to your competitors. First of all, you must understand your customers' needs.

When I opened my clinic in 2006, there were no other walk-in clinics in the area. After about three years, the area in which I lived has been showered with quite a few walk-in clinics here and there. We noticed our numbers dwindling. I spent quite a bit of time pondering the situation. Then I came up with a plan.

I started free monthly "Lunch and Learn" lectures at the clinic open to anyone willing to attend. We had a great response. Free food and free education? People loved and appreciated the information they received. With time, more and more of them signed up to start seeing us regularly.

Four areas of marketing include

1. **Your product/ service:** What product or service do you offer? Why is your product or service relevant? What are you trying to accomplish? What will you offer to your current and potential customers that they will trust, be aware of, and that will create a positive lasting sentiment? In other words, your customers should find your product or service extraordinary.

2. **Your competition:** What sets you apart? What is your unique selling proposition? This should be clear. What is your unique area of excellence? How do you convey this to your customer? Who are your current competitors? What are their advantages? What are your customers worried about?

3. **Your customer:** Who are your customers? Describe your ideal customer. What motivates your ideal customer? Where are they located? Are you reaching the decision maker? You must be crystal clear about what problem you solve with your customers. What is in the mind and heart of your ideal customer?

4. **Your modality:** What is the means to reach your ideal customer? TV, radio, Internet, face-to-face? You have to be able to communicate key facts about your products and services in a crystal-clear manner. How will you measure success? Set strict timelines. Constantly monitor the effectiveness of your marketing strategy. If it is not working, adjust it and try it again or drop it and try another.

There are several types of marketing modalities used now:

1. Direct marketing by "word of mouth"
2. Television
3. Radio
4. Billboards
5. Pinterest
6. Online social media
7. SEO optimization
8. Free samples
9. E-mail
10. Telemarketing

KEEPING UP WITH CHANGING TIMES

When I was in school, I remember the paper charts in which we had to handwrite everything pertaining to the patient. Handwritten patient documentation, medication orders, and nurses' instructions were the norm. Nowadays, computer-generated medical documentation is the norm. Ten or fifteen years ago, X-rays were taken onto a film which was developed then held up against a light, read, and stored. Nowadays, a processor can create a digital image which can be read by a specialist anywhere in the world.

For those of us in the healthcare, technology has become a revolution. It now influences how I, other physicians, and patients access and communicate healthcare information.

A patient comes in and the reason for him or her being here pops up on my screen. I sit on my desk for a few minutes. I look at their old progress notes and at all previous labs, X-rays, and treatments. With just a few clicks of a button, I can look at hospital records, pharmacy records, and records from other doctors, and within minutes, I am armed with a significant amount of pertinent medical information about this patient before I walk into the room and visit with them.

Forbes declared 2013 as the year of digital health. This means that the script for medical practice has been completely rewritten and it is no longer sufficient to be a competent medical professional to succeed. To succeed as a medical professional, you must also have the technology in place to keep your practice up to date with the new digital era. Choosing to ignore these technological advances as a medical professional will leave you behind and unable to match your medical expertise with proper and timely delivery of healthcare.

Rapidly advancing technology will now determine the future success of most businesses. Business owners must realize that their competition may be someone in a basement simply working on a laptop miles away. Entrepreneurs must shift their mind-set to focus on leveraging the proper technology to find their customers.

Brian J. Nichelson, PhD, in his article "Keeping up with Technology: Four Steps and Some Resources," outlined steps for individuals and businesses to take in order to keep up with changing technology. His reasoning is simple and practical. He states, "If you want to compete in today's business world, then, it's important to keep up with technology ..."

He summarizes that a good technology awareness strategy boils down to four simple steps.

1. Determine your needs.
2. Assess the resources available to you.
3. Rank the resources in order of usefulness to you.
4. Make or allow the time to use the resources.

I'll add two more steps to this.

5. Implement and train on the resources.
6. Maintain the technology and evaluate its effectiveness.

Let's look at a simple visual for the purpose of improving clarity.

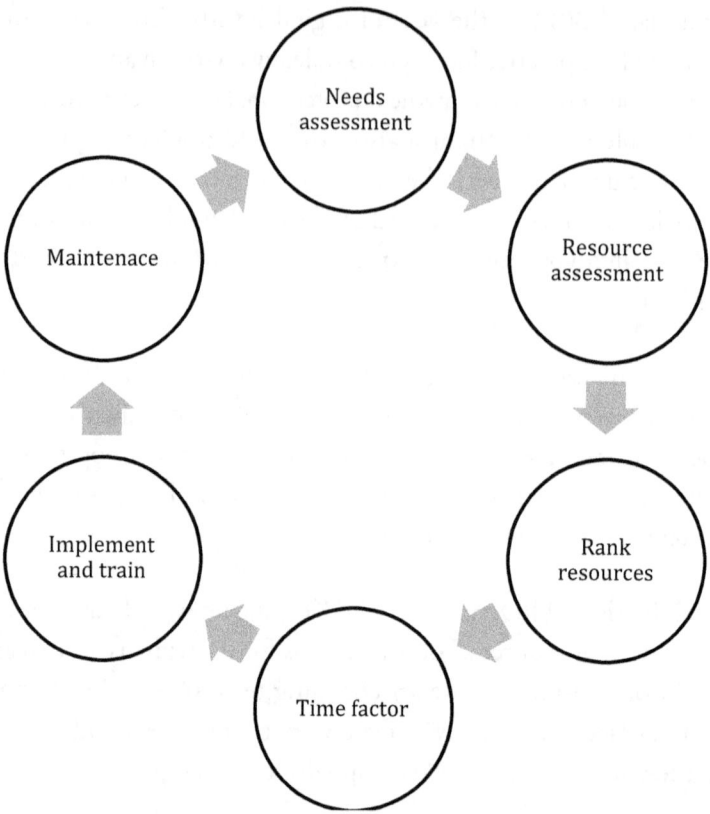

Business owners must be aware of the fact that, because of rapidly changing technology, the marketplace and competition are also changing.

Less than three years ago, to create a flyer for an event, I had on my list a handful of contacts I could get in touch with to have the job done. Today if I needed a flyer, I simply log into my computer and order one for less than 10 percent of the cost I paid three years ago.

There has been a shift to the mobile app usage and social media. Social media intelligence for all business owners is fast becoming a must. That is where most of your customers are. Social networking has now become an essential tool for businesses seeking competitive advantage.

Steps that gave my clinic a competitive advantage:

1. Electronic medical records
2. Digital X-rays
3. A company Facebook page
4. The patient portal allows patients to see certain aspects of their records.

Social media

Is defined as all the web applications and mobile apps that allow users the ability to connect and or share information.

Examples of social media:

Facebook
LinkedIn
Twitter
MySpace
StumbleUpon
Delicious
YouTube
Flickr
Digg
Reddit

EMPLOYEE MANAGEMENT

In 2012, Dale Carnegie teamed with MSW Research to study the functional and emotional elements that affect employee engagement.

According to their study, a national sample of 1,500 employees was surveyed, and three key factors that impacted employee engagement were identified. These are

- relationship with immediate supervisor
- belief in senior leadership
- pride in working for the company

This means that examining management practices is a key element in improving employee productivity. Note that employee compensation does not fall into these top three elements. Don't get me wrong. Employee compensation and benefits package are one of the key items examined by an employee as they seek employment. However, when it comes to factors influencing employee satisfaction, benefits and compensation are not rated high on the list.

Managing employees is not always a simple and straightforward task. If you are a business owner, manager, or supervisor you will definitely agree with this statement. There are so many details and intricacies in employee management that vary from organization to organization. The purpose of this segment is to give you a few tips on how to encourage and get more out of your employees as you move forward.

Being knowledgeable and friendly is one of the key qualities that your employees must hold to be able to keep the customer satisfied. It is also important for employers to invest in keeping their employees knowledgeable and friendly. Well-trained and friendlier employees add significant value to your customers and hence to your business. Employee satisfaction is one of the greatest motivation for employees. It is also a significant component of your customer satisfaction. So make sure you share customer contentment with your entire staff. Other factors like a friendly family environment are also important. Remember employees are the most valuable assets in your business.

Discipline and consistency are key factors that help maintain stability among employees in the workplace. Within any corporation, structure, goals, and positive feedback all help maintain employee satisfaction. Follow through with enforcing the rules, lead with a complement, and lead by example; don't always point out the problems. Make your demands reasonable. Listen to your employees. Encourage employees to make positive suggestions. Identify and recognize your employees' strengths. Provide ways for your employees to improve. Give employees their space. They need time to breathe so they can stay focused on the project. Don't be afraid to let an employee go. Studies show that retaining an employee who should be let go has significant negative consequences on your organization.

One of the main reasons why employees leave a company is because they feel unappreciated.

Creating a workplace environment or an atmosphere that improves their well-being or the emotional state of your employees will ultimately improve the customer experience.

Let's briefly look at ways to boost your employee satisfaction.

1. Make each employee's anniversary with your company an achievement and a special occasion. When employee anniversaries are celebrated, coworkers are excited and overall employee morale is boosted. Employee happiness is critical to the success of your business.

2. Employee motivation, a path for growth, and a flexible family work environment also build the strength of a small, family-oriented company.

3. Turnover is not necessary a bad thing. So it is important to get the bad employees out of the company so that they do not destroy your company.

4. An employee handbook is one of the first introductions that an employee will have to the general policies and procedures in a company. Make sure your employee handbook gives clear and precise guidelines on expectations from your employees. Most large companies or businesses should have an employee management committee or a human resources department.

Now let's look at tips on improving your employee productivity.

1. Ensure adequate new employee orientation.
2. Provide meaningful feedback.
3. Provide your employees adequate tools to perform their jobs.
4. Train employees on a safe work environment.
5. Design employee incentives.
6. Keep employees and managers accountable.
7. Identify areas that need improvement.
8. Identify areas for employee advancement.
9. Keep your employees informed and educated about new products.
10. Share performance data.
11. Allow some flexibility with work hours.
12. Train employees on how to handle difficult customers.
13. Invest in formal training programs.
14. Model the behavior you want to see in your employees.

We cannot conclude the topic on employee management without talking about employee competence and skill training.

When we talk about competence, most of the time we believe that this pertains to the workplace only. However, we also have to consider social competence. Social competence is a little more abstract and refers to social, emotional communication and behavioral skills as well as our expectations. For the purposes of this book we will focus on competence on the job.

Skills Training

The success of any business or corporation is highly dependent on having well-trained, skilled, and competent employees. While most organizations spend a great deal of time in the training of their new employees, the majority of businesses fail by not continuing to provide education and instruction to their employees on a regular basis throughout the course of their professional career. Most licensed personnel in the medical field must be continuously educated before they are qualified to renew their licenses. This keeps the medical professional competent, skilled, and abreast with the ever-changing medical information.

The take-home message here is that every corporation must provide some form of ongoing skill training for their employees in order to maintain or improve their job performance.

Competency and Effectiveness

Every employee is skilled to a certain degree. If a business or corporation is not employing proper skill-training techniques to achieve some minimum level of effectiveness, then the business may be doomed to fail. Ineffective skill-training instruction of employees will ultimately waste valuable talent of these individuals.

Skills Training and Competency

Having a well-trained and competent staff is absolutely necessary in order to run a business, but this does not mean that success in business will be guaranteed to succeed.

Having a staff of poorly trained employees will immediately damage your business as well as your professional reputation. However, simply employing well-trained staff will not necessarily improve the bottom line.

It is simply not enough to employ a staff of individuals with high levels of competence and training; they must possess the ability to work together as a team. For example, within the National Basketball Association are professional teams filled with hundreds of players who routinely exhibit great levels of competence, skill, and drive. Yet very few of these teams are ultimately successful in winning titles. Each team must focus on training the players to work successfully as a team in order for that team to win.

An African proverb says, "If you want to go quickly, go alone; if you want to go far, go together."

This proverb speaks for itself.

Job Performance

Another common mistake that many businesses make is in the method in which a regular employee is rated on their annual job performance reviews. Many employers focus more on what the employees *do not do* rather than what they *cannot do*. Put another way, not all employees are capable of the same things. Every employee has his or her own individual strengths and weaknesses. It is the job of management to build a team that complements the skills set of each individual employee—ultimately building a team that gets results. The focus should be on the optimum levels of competence for the team as opposed to the individual.

Skills-Training Tips

1. Make sure that each employee has a clear and measurable set of standards that will dictate their overall job performance and efficiency.

2. Put systems in place that will make it nearly impossible for your staff to fail. If your internal systems are poor, then the levels of competence and skill of your individual employees really won't matter.

3. Encourage system improvements from your staff. Get your employees to buy into the system.

4. Create reward systems not only for singular employees but for successful teams as well. Take the focus off of the individual and replace it with a focus on the overall success of a larger department or of the company as a whole.

SECTION 3:
PERSEVERANCE

Perseverance

Perseverance or persistence, tenacity, steadfastness, is defined in *Merriam-Webster's Collegiate Dictionary* as continued effort to do or achieve something despite difficulties, failure, or opposition.

To achieve personal success, one must be consistent and persevere regardless of all the obstacles that may slow us down.

In 2003, while in my second-year family medicine residency program, I made up my mind that upon my graduation from residency, I would start up my own private medical practice. I imagined it would be a difficult choice, but I was convinced that this is what I wanted to do. When I graduated from residency, I immediately started working as an emergency room physician but I held on to my dream. When my world was shaken and I was down and out because of illness, I still maintained that faith in the dream.

Today, after several successes and innumerable challenges and mistakes—some small and others gigantic and painful—I have learned several lessons on perseverance. I will share them here with you in order to help you persevere and stay on your chosen path to greatness.

To be successful, you must persevere. You must continue to do the things that work and develop them. At the same time, you must be brave and bold enough to stop doing the things that don't work.

I believe the definition of insanity quoted by Albert Einstein: doing the same thing repeatedly and expecting to get different results.

Here are my top seven perseverance lessons:

1. Practice makes persistence.
2. Giving up is not an option.
3. Be flexible only for long enough to redirect the course.

4. Mistakes are part of the process.
5. Be careful with finances.
6. Get creative.
7. Get out of your comfort zone.

LEADERSHIP

Leadership has been described as "a process by which a person influences others toward the accomplishment of a common goal. The late Peter Drucker, hailed by *Business Week* as "the man who invented management," states that business owners and managers must realize that they are the most important salesperson on the team. Therefore, leaders must cultivate the power to influence people.

> "Leadership is not about titles, positions, or flowcharts.
> It is about one life influencing another." "Leadership
> is influence, nothing more, nothing less."
> —John C. Maxwell

As owner and CEO of my own company since 2006, I have learned that being a good leader has a wide scope of demands and skills that go beyond any formal training curriculum. Being an expert in your field, having a great vision, and having good intentions are just not enough. Even working hard, diligently, and consistently is just not good enough either.

Leaders should be willing to place themselves in the fire of ever-changing demands, develop courage and strong character, and embody the character of complete dedication to the purpose and the determination to keep on keeping on. You need to develop abilities to face challenges and handle all kinds of situations. Your experiences will sharpen you every day.

As I write this book, I am the president of my alumni association. This experience has sharpened further my leadership skills. It has given me the strength of character to withstand adversity and distractions and stay the course no matter what.

I was not born a leader. With time, I learned to become a leader. Some people are born with leadership capabilities and others are not.

My top ten qualities of a good leader are the following:

1. Courage
2. Communication
3. Influence
4. Honesty
5. Humility
6. Knowledge
7. Steadfastness
8. Integrity
9. Positive attitude
10. Being inspirational

Leadership requires personal strength and development. One of the key qualities of being a great leader is to communicate effectively with others. By practicing active listening, paying attention to body language, and developing social awareness, you will certainly grow and develop your leadership skills.

Acquiring or developing leadership qualities will award your tenacity when it comes to staying the course. In other words, in order to persevere through life's curveballs inside and outside of work, you should develop some leadership skills to help you along. That is why the leaders of the organization are ones who have the capability to take the organization one step further. They are the ones who are passionate about their work. They know how to dream big and have the passion to chase after that dream.

PERSONAL IMPROVEMENT

Next, there is self-improvement. Self-improvement is described in *Wikipedia* as "self-guided improvement—economically, intellectually, or emotionally." Meaning that it is by your own actions and efforts that your knowledge and abilities improve. Les Parrot, founder of the Center for Relationship Development in Seattle Pacific University states, "If you want to win with people you have got to be a winner yourself—or at the very least be on your way to becoming one."

Personal improvement requires deliberate thought, planning, and recognizing the fact that any skill or action requires consistency and commitment over time in order to be mastered. It is also important to break down a set goal into small steps, for example.

No matter where you are in life, no matter your educational level, your personal sense of accomplishment, you have room for improvement. Take inventory of yourself and identify areas that you need to improve.

As a family medicine physician, I counsel people every day on weight loss. Regardless of how much weight you have to lose to get to your ideal weight and maintain it, the steps to get there are the same. You must make daily healthy food choices and exercise routinely. Let's say you have one hundred pounds to lose. It sure sounds like an impossible goal. However, if you focus on losing one to two pounds weekly as recommended by the experts, over time, you will not only achieve your goal but you would have learned new healthy habits that are now a part of your lifestyle.

I strongly believe that developing oneself is one of the most important steps a person can take and that personal improvement ultimately leads to more achievements in one's life than anything else.

Remember that each of us was born with limitless potential. Thus, there is no limit to personal improvement. We must seek to grow and improve endlessly regardless of our circumstances.

Self-control is one of the greatest attributes to cultivate when it comes to self-improvement. This is the one of the best examples for others, our children, those who work with us, and everyone else around us to know that we are in control of our emotions.

According to John Maxwell, growth doesn't just happen. "Growth is essential to our satisfaction and our success, but it doesn't just happen." It means that you must take the time to study hard to develop yourself and to grow personally. It will not happen spontaneously. It happens only on purpose. You should have a plan for personal growth. No one ever grows by accident. John Maxwell goes on to say, "The greatest gap in the world in the gap between knowing and doing."

Self-motivation is a helpful skill to master when it comes to self-improvement.

Have you ever heard of the saying "You are your own worst enemy"? If you lose steam in life or allow your thoughts to be crowded by too much negativity, your effectiveness and your ability to excel will be dampened.

I have an acronym: MIND. It stands for **m**ental **i**nsight **n**urtures **d**evelopment. The mind is the most powerful organ in your body! It can make you feel sick when you are physically healthy, so keeping a healthy mind is important. Successful people like Mother Teresa, MLK, Gandhi, and JFK all portrayed personalities with healthy mind-sets. Like everything else in life, acquiring and keeping a healthy mind can be achieved through self-motivation.

Tips That Helped Me with Self-Motivation

A critical component to achieving the life of your dreams is to become very aware of your self-motivation and how it impacts the quality of your life with regards to professional achievements, personal relationships, and individual goals.

Learning how to manage your attitude to its highest rate of effectiveness will enhance your life in all regards.

Self-Motivation Strategies

1. Use affirmations.

Stay positive! It's easier said than done, but make an effort to consciously stay positive, and then with time (if you have not cultivated a lifelong habit of negativity), it will get easier.

Take time to write and recite repetitive affirmations to yourself several times a day to aid in reprogramming your mind! Make sure that your affirmation is charged with power and positivity. Don't say, "I want to be successful." Instead, say, "I *am* successful." Don't say, "I want to have a good day today." Instead, say, "Today is a *great day* with lots of productivity!" Say it with a smile on your face while looking in the mirror. Your subconscious mind will only believe what you tell it to believe.

2. Know your passion.

Know yourself! What excites you? What motivates you to take charge of your life and make changes? Are your motives based on love, anger, financial reward, fear, power, self-protection, compassion, service, or empathy? What makes you enthusiastic and energetic? What makes you smile or makes your heart skip a beat? Self-motivation requires passion! Passion will help you overcome most of your fears and believe in your God-given abilities.

1. Visualization. If you can think it, you can achieve it. This may sound somewhat simplistic, but many psychological studies have proven that many engineers, artists, athletes, and business moguls use either conscious or unconscious acts of visualizations and affirmations to focus their energies on a given goal. Nelson Mandela was imprisoned for some twenty-seven years and made public that his ability to visualize enhanced his spirits and instilled great hope. He is famously quoted in his autobiography as saying, "I thought continually of the day when I would walk free. I fantasized about what I would like to do." Nelson Mandela eventually became a free man and became president of South Africa.

2. "Attitude Talk". This method is used to replace those negative statements that are floating around inside your head with a more positive and forward-thinking inner voice. It can help to erase the past negative programming, install new productive images, and create a new direction for personal power. Listen to your inner dialogue as often as you can each day. What is that little voice really saying to you?

3. Watch your words. Become more aware of the words that you speak, for once they are released, they can never be recalled! How we speak to others around us is a direct reflection of how we are feeling inside. If we are reacting harshly or disparagingly toward those around us, perhaps it is time to look deep within to see what it is that is making us feel so badly. Do you feel powerless? Are you fearful? If so, what are you afraid of? Get in touch with that inner dialogue and see what is making you tick! Then *choose* to create self-motivation by first changing your words!

4. Be enthusiastic. Enthusiasm is the gasoline in the automobile of life! Enthusiasm drives our motivation, steers our determination, guides our ambition, and powers our commitment. It is one of the most attractive qualities found in others. Try living your life with enthusiasm! Whatever task you are doing, no matter how trivial or insignificant, try forcing yourself to address the assignment with

zest and vigor! Paste a smile on your face. Say, "I get to …" instead of "I have to …" This is a wonderful method of reprogramming your brain!

5. Exercise.Being active has so many positive effects on the body, mind, and spirit. Many studies show that students actually are better able to concentrate after a good dose of physical activity. Ever hear of recess? It is also a well-known fact that exercise releases endorphins in your brain, which leads to a more enthusiastic attitude and an enhanced euphoric mental state. You also might gain some additional exciting side effects, such as weight loss, increased muscle mass, and better fitting clothes, which all lead to higher self-esteem.

Let's visualize these strategies to stay motivated.

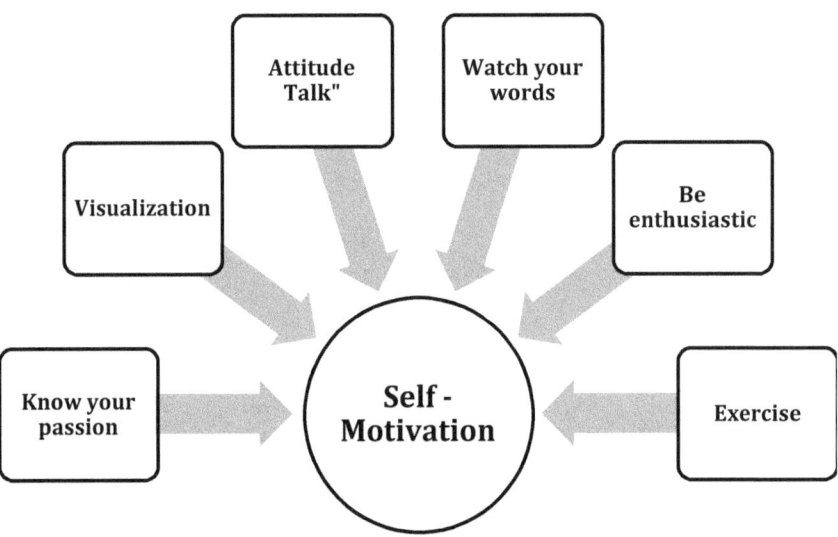

Get your life back on track and create a road to success and personal achievement by adopting these simple tools. Start looking at life differently and adopt a position of positivity! Increase your self-motivation, and it may eventually change your life!

Important areas of personal improvement that have been very helpful for me include the following:

1. Spiritual growth
2. Weight loss
3. Improving listening skills
4. Communicating more effectively
5. Increasing self-love
6. Physical fitness
7. Getting involved in charitable activities
8. Setting goals for myself
9. Avoiding negative people
10. Getting a coach
11. Stopping watching TV
12. Letting go of the past
13. Making time for family

RELATIONSHIPS

Merriam-Webster's Collegiate Dictionary defines relationships as the way in which two or more people, groups, countries, etc., talk to, behave toward, and deal with each other.

The relationships we nurture, and how we interact with the people we come in contact with, speak of who we are. Close and positive relationships lead to numerous positive mental and physical changes within us, and a general sense of well-being. In this same light, be careful about the relationships that you keep close to you. Some relationships are nourishing and help you grow and excel. Other relationships are toxic and limit your ability to succeed. Make every effort to turn away from toxic relationships. A list of relationships generally includes a life companion (spouse, mate, etc.), friends, family members, coworkers, and so forth.

There are specific types of relationships in my experience to be on the lookout for, including these:

1. Healthy relationships. Nurture these.
2. Unhealthy relationships. Reevaluate your need for these.
3. New relationships. Seek these.

As your journey of personal growth continues, you should develop new relationships, especially those that will help you *Grow to Success*.

Ten Steps to Developing Healthy Relationships

1. Know yourself.
2. Be respectful.
3. Be giving, not always receiving.
4. Nurture your relationships.
5. Be accepting of the other person's perspective.
6. Watch your words and take responsibility for them.
7. Communicate your thoughts.
8. Don't bring stress into your relationships.
9. Be a good listener.
10. Be honest.

FAITH AND MOTIVATION

Staying motivated on my purpose and believing that my dream will be of valuable service to others has been one of the drives for me personally. How do high achievers like Bill Gates, Steve Jobs, Tiger Woods, Serena Williams, and Earvin (Magic) Johnson achieve success? What is it that sets these people apart from the rest of us? Listening to and studying their bios, you hear these successful people talk over and over about aiming high, staying motivated, being persistent enough to overcome obstacles, and working hard.

Staying motivated and having faith in your dream will set and keep you on the path to success.

Ten Steps to Stay Motivated in Accomplishing Your Goals and Your Dreams

1. Dream and dream big.
2. Identify your goal.
3. Research and study.
4. Step out of your comfort zone.
5. Shake off the negativity.
6. Make a plan and put your plan into action.
7. Enjoy your achievements.
8. Be persistent.
9. Believe in yourself.
10. Be consistent.

> *"Now **faith** is the substance of things hoped*
> for, *the evidence of things not seen."*
> Hebrews 11:1 (King James Version)

I believe that faith represents the truth revealed in God's Word, the Bible. I also believe that the church presents the truth to us as a set of rules and regulations by which good Christian habits and principles lie in the foundation.

My Christian values are at the core of my being, and my faith in God has helped me along the way. I strive to reach to God daily and maintain a close relationship with Him. He has helped me in times of need and in times of sorrow. At this point, I can only encourage you to seek and know God for yourself. He will never fail you. Make it a habit to read the Word of God daily and live by His principles.

In order to survive the wear and tear on ourselves because of our activities of daily living, it is helpful to develop a reasonable mind-body routine geared at self-preservation. In this chapter, I will share with you some tips which have helped me persevere through the years.

a. Faith

Faith is defined in *Merriam-Webster's Collegiate Dictionary* as an allegiance to duty or a person. Other definitions include loyalty, fidelity to one's promises, sincerity of intentions, belief, and trust in and loyalty to God or in the traditional doctrines of a religion.

So you see, the definition of faith is not exclusive to religion. It simply specifies the belief in something intangible without physical evidence. We all have faith because we perform tasks daily that could be life threatening. For example, if you drive down the street, you must have faith in all other drivers. However, when it comes to an idea or a goal, most people will look for tangible proof of success before taking any steps to make them become a reality.

"Now faith is the substance of things hoped for,
the evidence of things not seen."
Hebrews 11:1 (NKJV)

I first entered medical school in Monrovia, Liberia. This journey was cut short only after three months by a brutal civil war. After witnessing multiple despicable human acts, I was blessed to be one of the last people to be able to fly out of the only airport in the capital city of Monrovia. I returned to my home country Cameroon. At the age of twenty-one, I possessed a bachelor's degree in biochemistry, a discipline that I loathed. I had a desire in my heart to become a medical doctor. Thinking back, I never lost faith in my dream. I spent a lot of time thinking about how to get into a medical school. I spent hours in the library researching medical schools. I discussed multiple plans with my parents. In the end, I chose to leave my country and travel to Italy to start medical school. This was a bold but necessary step in achieving my dream. You see, even the civil war could not quench my dream. I knew that I would go to Italy and leave Italy after six years with my medical degree, and as tough as it was, I made it. I always had the faith that I would succeed, and that was very important. It never occurred to me at any point in my life that I would not achieve my dream profession.

So when you have a goal and a dream, make sure you keep the faith that you can achieve it, regardless of life's curveballs; believe in yourself. So long as your dream or goal is acceptable within the realms of the law, and of society, keep the faith.

Don't let yourself or anyone else talk you out of your dream. Teach your children the same. Faith is a fundamental attribute to possess and is one of the keys to your success. How we feed our faith leads me to my next point: prayer.

Prayer

The following passages on prayer are based on my personal believes as a Christian. I share these because the power of prayer has seen me through many formidable trials of life. It is a very important tool to have and to use, and it will see you through life's trials, tribulations, jubilations, and celebrations.

Prayer is not only asking God when we want something. It is in fact communion with the Almighty Father. We converse with God because he is our father, friend, and soul mate. And like in conversation, it is not always about asking but thanksgiving too. It comes out of love, faith, and belief. In short, we can say prayer is life, it is love, it is the breath of our soul, and it is our birthright. The Bible says, "Ask, and it will be given to you; seek, and you will find; knock, and it will be opened to you" (Matthew 7:7 NKJV).

Why pray?

Why should we pray when God knows everything? Doesn't God give everything without partiality? But one more fact is that even a mother grants something to the child that asks or begs. Then why will not the heavenly Father? Does that mean that the child who does not ask loses? No. The person who doesn't ask also receives even more than he or she would have asked.

What should we pray for?

It is natural for a person to ask, in the times of distress, for things that he needs. But here we forget when God knows everything, wouldn't He know our sorrows? The state that we feel as sorrow is the test that God takes to help us develop our virtues. So if we have to ask, we should pray for other's well-being. We should pray for our self-development and qualities of a good human being. Pray to God with all your heart and soul, and then gather up all your might to meet those challenges that lie ahead in the world.

Power of prayer

The power of prayer should not be underestimated. Prayers can even bring mountains down. In James 5:16 (NKJV), we read, "Confess *your* trespasses to one another, and pray for one another, that you may be healed. The effective, fervent prayer of a righteous man avails much." The prayer of a righteous man is powerful and effective.

RECREATION

A man has to learn that he cannot command things, but that he can command himself; that he cannot coerce the wills of others, but that he can mold and master his own will: and things serve him who serves Truth; people seek guidance of him who is master of himself.
—James Allen

Merriam-Webster's Collegiate Dictionary defines recreation as something people do to relax or have fun; activities done for enjoyment; refreshment of strength and spirits after work; a means of refreshment or diversion.

You know what they say about "all work and no play." You are the master of yourself. In order to be successful, one must train oneself to find a balance between work and recreation. Set aside time from work to enjoy leisurely activities in order to refresh mind and body. To be more efficient, learn to take step away from work and life's obligations so that you can recharge your energies.

Recreational activities like sports, have been associated with multiple positive outcomes, such as increased physical activity and lower stress levels. During recreation, overcoming a goal one previously thought of as impossible leads to improved self-esteem and self-confidence. Community and group recreational activities have been shown to reduce crime rates and develop leadership abilities through teamwork.

Recreation also helps improve relationships and can give you the opportunity to form new acquaintances.

Physical activities like walking, jogging, cycling, fishing, and other outdoor activities can be relaxing, refreshing, and energizing.

More and more people are finding it challenging to strike a proper work-life balance. Increasing technology that allow access to work while away from work, increased responsibility, life demands, and more beyond our control simply have our days so packed it may seem impossible to squeeze in time for recreation.

Here are some tips that helped me add recreation to my daily life:

1. Planning. Be intentional about adding recreation to your daily schedule.
2. Time management. Effective time management helps create more time for recreation.
3. Eliminate unnecessary activities that sap your time and energy.
4. Don't wait for a "huge time block to be available." Work with what you have.
5. Learn to say no to things that are thrown at you that you cannot handle.

Examples of recreational activities that help me recharge:

1. Walking, jogging, running
2. Reading
3. Zumba
4. Writing
5. Traveling
6. Music
7. Dancing

HEALTHY LIFESTYLE CHANGES

The World Health Organization (WHO) defines health as a state of complete physical, mental, and social well-being, not simply just the absence of disease.

To be successful in life, to be able to pursue your goals and dreams, whatever they may be, you must make every effort to put yourself in a place of optimum health by taking care of your body, your emotions, and your relationships, or else you will not go very far.

Adopting a healthy lifestyle is certainly not easy. If you think about it in its entirety, it sounds like an enormous feat. However, breaking it down into small steps makes it achievable. All you have to do is incorporate the steps, one at a time, into your daily life consistently over time.

Change will not happen overnight. It will involve dedication and consistency. It will involve you taking responsibility for your daily food choices, for your exercise habits, for your mind-set, and for your interactions with others.

No matter where you are in life, it is never too soon or too late to make a commitment toward healthy living.

Scientific evidence shows that living a healthy lifestyle significantly reduces our risk of developing many chronic health problems. These include diseases like hypertension, high cholesterol, heart disease, cancer, diabetes, joint disease, and mental illness, which not only impact our quality of life but can also reduce our life expectancy.

So you are reading this book because you want to be successful, right? So let's get smart and incorporate healthy living into our daily routine. Ignoring a healthy lifestyle may potentially and drastically reduce your chances and your ability to *Grow to Success!*

My personal experience with the challenge of keeping my weight close to ideal has taught me that healthy living has to be a lifelong commitment of awareness of the choices you make daily or else you start to back slide into old bad habits.

So moving forward, there are a few tips that helped me live mindfully and make better choices to achieve and improve my health.

1. Change your mind-set. It starts with you. You make the choice. Give yourself a reality check. Only you have the power to believe in yourself and take the necessary steps.
2. Set goals long and short term.
3. Set up an accountability system.
4. Exercise three to four times a week.
5. Stop smoking.
6. Eat five to six small healthy meals daily.
7. Work toward a healthy weight.
8. Know your numbers: blood pressure, blood sugar, and blood cholesterol.
9. Reduce stress.
10. Plan your meals.

Eat a variety of fruits, vegetables, and whole grains every day. Limit foods and drinks high in calories, sugar, salt, fat, and alcohol.

Wellness

Wellness is generally used to mean a healthy balance of the mind, body, and spirit that results in an overall feeling of well-being. Wellness is achieved by learning and putting to practice relevant health and wellness actions on a long-term basis. I hope you can use some of the wellness tips mentioned here to help you achieve your health and wellness goals.

Staying healthy can be challenging; however, making simple, wise choices daily and consistently will set and keep you on the right path to a healthy lifestyle change.

Strategies to help you accomplish your wellness goals:

1. Eat healthy.

Heart disease is the no. 1 killer of Americans. According to The American Heart Association, "We can reduce heart disease by promoting a healthy diet and lifestyle. Getting information from credible sources can help you make smart choices that will benefit your long-term heart health." According to The American Heart Association, as part of a healthy diet, an adult consuming 2,000 calories daily should aim for

- fruits and vegetables: at least four to five cups a day
- fish (preferably oily fish): at least two three- to five-ounce servings a week
- fiber-rich whole grains: at least three one-ounce-equivalent servings a day
- sodium: less than 1,500 mg a day
- sugar-sweetened beverages: no more than 450 calories (thirty-six ounces) a week

Other Dietary Measures

- nuts, legumes, and seeds: at least four servings a week
- processed meats: no more than two servings a week
- saturated fat: less than 7 percent of total energy intake

If you drink alcohol, do so in moderation. This means an average of one to two drinks per day for men and one drink per day for women. (A drink is one twelve-ounce beer, four-ounce glass of wine, 1.5-ounce glass of eighty-proof spirits, or one ounce of one-hundred-proof spirits.)

2. Exercise regularly.

Exercise improves blood flow and releases natural substances that have multiple health benefits. For physical fitness, one should follow an exercising schedule daily. It need not be in a gym.

- Be active for at least two to three hours a week. Try not to skip more than two consecutive days without exercising.
- Combinations of activities that raise your heart rates and that strengthen your muscles are most helpful.

The benefits of exercise are well documented and include

a. reducing the incidence of heart disease
b. reducing your risk of diabetes and hypertension
c. reducing your risk of stroke
d. reducing your risk of cancer
e. maintaining a healthy weight
f. maintaining healthy bones and joints
g. reducing arthritis pain and associated disability
h. reducing symptoms of depression and anxiety

3. Manage stress.

- Balance your time at work, time with family, and time for recreational activities.
- Stay positive.
- Take time to relax.
- Get seven to nine hours of sleep each night.
- Get help or counseling if needed.

4. Get regular check-ups.

- Regular check-ups can discover diseases before they are gone far enough to cause complications. Check with your medical provider regarding what exams, tests, and shots you need and when to get them.
- Get seen if you notice changes in your body or fall ill. Get a check-up immediately.

Sleep well.

Adults should get seven to nine hours daily, whereas school-aged children should get ten to eleven. Proper sleeping habits will keep your mind alert for, as the saying goes, "Early to bed and early to rise makes a man healthy, wealthy, and wise."

6. Improve your psychological and social health.

It is important to feel good about ourselves and the world around us, to be able to get the most out of our lives. When we talk about good health, we mean good physical, emotional, and social health. It is therefore important to develop meaningful relationships above simply being social. Practice self-disclosure, which means sharing things that are unique to you. Practice maintaining a healthy attitude through life's curveballs.

In Conclusion

In writing this book, I hope to inspire you into believing in yourself. Have a passion, have a dream. Martin Luther King had a dream. Why can't we all have a dream like that? It's a trick question; we all can. But we limit ourselves to hopes, desires, even aspirations, but we cut it there and say, "No, I'm not strong enough to have a dream. No, I am not smart enough to have a dream. No, I am not outgoing enough to have a dream. No, I am not pretty enough to have a dream. No, I am not confident enough to have a dream. I am not worthy enough to have a dream. My lack of education stops me from having a dream. My job stops me from having a dream. My life is not worthy of a dream."

Everyone has a reason. It's an excuse. We *all* can dream of a brighter future, and not just that, but we can act toward it and accomplish it. We have the power to make it a reality. So even though we often feel as though it's set in stone, all it takes is a *dreamer* to change it all. Have a dream. And then put yourself through a process of growth. Success requires growth. *Grow to Success.*

"Seven Steps to Success by John C. Maxwell"

1) Make a commitment to grow daily.
2) Value the process more than events.
3) Don't wait for inspiration.
4) Be willing to sacrifice pleasure for opportunity.
5) Dream big.
6) Plan your priorities.
7) Give up to go up.

No matter where you are in life, focus on achieving your dream regardless of your circumstances. You have the God-given ability to be successful. Find your passion! Set your personal bar high, make a plan, work hard, and go through the growth process. *Grow to Success.* You can do it!

Notes:

GROW TO SUCCESS WORKBOOK

A set of skills that taught me to achieve personal and professional success!

CONTENTS

Success is not about wealth. It is not about the size of your bank account or your education. It is not about your age or position. Success is a personal sense of accomplishment, that you have succeeded in finding and accomplishing your God-given purpose.

In this workbook, you will find the "action points" extracted from the book itself as well as several practical exercises and worksheets that will help you practice, review, and master the content of the book.

Keep these notes and refer to them often. Notes help you remember and keep you on track.

GOALS

Definition: A goal is the _____ __ a person's _____ or

_____; an aim or _____ _____.

Focus on the emotional aspect of the goal and on the end in mind. You must have an end in mind.

Ask yourself how you will *feel* if you accomplish this goal.

You must find your why, a reason why you want to achieve this goal.

Be crystal clear about your goal, and then make a plan to achieve it.

Practice the acronym for the criteria used in goal setting: the **SMARTER** criteria.

S_____

M_____

A_____

R_____

T_____

E_____

R_____

Goal-Setting Exercise

Now with the SMARTER criteria in mind, spend some time thinking about your goals and where they will take you.

Next write down three to five goals.

1.

2.

3.

4.

5.

Now write down five reasons why you chose these goals.

1.

2.

3.

4.

5.

When it comes to the _____ and _____ of an organization, it will take a _____ to guide and direct the team toward successful accomplishment of the goals and the mission.

Who has the ability to influence the entire team toward the accomplishment of the organization's goals?_____

Write down ten important qualities of a good leader. How many of these do you possess?

!.

2.

3.

4.

5.

6.

7.

8.

9.

10.

KNOWLEDGE ACQUISITION

Why is the purposeful acquisition of the knowledge and skills that you need to understand the basics of accomplishing this goals important?

You need to _____ in _____ in order to place yourself on a path of continuous learning.

Remember you cannot outgrow yourself. So you must expand your knowledge in order to grow.

Acquire knowledge in ten easy steps:

1. **Exposure**

2. **Input control**

3. **Research**

4. **Do it daily**

5. **Spend time thinking.**

6. **Positive mind-set.**

7. **Consistency**

8. **Time management**

9. **Invest in yourself.**

10. **Listen and observe**

Notes:

PLAN

If you don't plan your steps to achieve your goal, you will find yourself walking off on a tangent and in the end miss your target!

Why plan?

- Work it out clearly.
- Think about how.
- Work out any extra support.
- Examine your life.
- Think about the plan B.
- Think about adjustments.
- Plan to make these changes.
- Write down your thoughts.

Specific knowledge that helped me lead my business to success:

1. Skills set.

Every leader must have the _____ in the specific field or industry. They must be able to bring into the organization team members that possess needed skills that the leader may not possess.

A good leader must _____ the _____they expect to see in the rest of the team.

2. Teamwork.

So a good leader should understand ____ _____ of each team member and fit them in the position where they can _____ and _____ grow and excel.

3. Be adaptable to change.

The leader must be _____ enough to let in new ideas and concepts brought in by the team members.

_____ training of the team is another marketable skill which is a must have and teach the team members.

4. Be a good leader. A good leader _____ the _____.

5. Create other leaders. This is one of the most _____ skill set you must acquire knowledge in.

COMMITMENT

He who would accomplish little need sacrifice little; he who would achieve much must sacrifice much. He who would attain highly must sacrifice greatly.
—James Allen, As a Man Thinketh

Commitment is a promise to do or give something.

Tips to improve commitment

Stay Engaged.

_____

Stay positive.

_____

Stay excited.

_____

Foster relationships.

_____

Stay connected.

_____

Foster Empowerment.

_____

What is organizational commitment? Why is it important?

There are three types of organizational commitment.

1. Normative commitment

This involves a sense of _____ to the _____ and causes employees to feel a sense of _____to stay whether they are happy or not.

2. Affective commitment

Is the _____ _____ of an employee to organizational values. The employee stays with the company because their goals line up with those of the organization's and because of this their choose to remain in employment.

3. Continuance commitment

Is a _____ of the employees' _____ to staying with the company even if the conditions become less than ideal.

Name five ways you can improve your commitment.

1.

2.

3.

4.

5.

PERSONAL DEVELOPMENT

It's a *process* of improving and growing one's awareness, skills, abilities.

Develop yourself before you can ever be able to become the person that you want to be.

Growth is not _____. "The greatest gap in the world is the gap between _____ and _____."
                        —John Maxwell

"People are anxious to improve their circumstances but are unwilling to improve themselves. They therefore remain bound."
                        —James Allen

The *big three controls* of personal development

1. **Your thoughts**

   Positive thinking_____ _____ the internal environment within you for personal development.

2. **Your relationships**

   Most of our relationships are social ones. Some relationships are _____and others are _____

3. **Your network**

   Make an effort to _____ our _____relationships by simply _____ with and collaborating with other like-minded people.

List your five big areas of personal development.

1.

2.

3.

4.

5.

What is your personal development plan?

GOAL DRIVEN

Imagine the _____ _____ or a desired _____. Imagine yourself _____ _____ to get to that end point or result. That's the meaning of goal driven.

A simple way of looking at this is that you cannot get to where you're trying to go until you clearly define where it is that you are going.

Maintaining_____and in _____ in the process to achieve that goal will keep you goal oriented. In so doing, you can become an expert at whatever it is that you are focusing on. Strive to see the end in your mind.

Strategies to stay focused on a goal

- Set clear goals.
- Make a specific plan.
- Set timelines.
- Prioritize.
- Stay focused.
- Track progress.
- Celebrate goal achievement.

In an organization, it's up to the _____ to have _____ in place for keeping the team _____on achieving the goal thus the _____ of the company itself.

The steps for keeping everyone in a company engaged and focused on the goal are similar.

- Define clear _____in line with the mission of the company.
- Establish the _____ to achieve the goals.
- Set realistic _____.

- Review _____ regularly.
- Accountability.
- Monitor_____.
- _____/ bonuses.

Notes:

FOCUS

The lack of focus and the multitude of _____ we have within and around us will _____ your _____ to achieve success.

It is impossible to focus on _____things at a time.

So you must become very _____on what you allow your mind to stay _____ on.

Maintaining _____is one of the key _____that will allow you to _____ success.

A leader's ability to _____brings forth the aspects of _____and _____within the organization.

Notes:

Things That Will Interrupt Your Focus

1. Social media
2. Mobile phones/text messages
3. Television/loud music
4. Intrusive thoughts
5. Poor or lack of planning
6. Lack of clear goals and expectations
7. Lack of proper skills

What is your plan to improve your ability to stay focused? Write down your plan and make a decision to follow this plan daily.

Notes:

Staying Focused Tips

1. **Plan and prioritize.**

2. **Focus and awareness.**

3. **Narrow your focus.**

4. **Eliminate external distractions.**

5. **Eliminate internal distractions.**

A healthy lifestyle is _____. Avoid mind-altering _____like prescription _____ _____, _____ _____, and _____.

Develop healthy habits, such as proper _____, _____ with water and regular _____.

If you are reading this book and admit that you are addicted to any mind-altering substances, I urge you to seek immediate help. Your health is paramount to success.

MIND-SET DEVELOPMENT

The mind-set can be defined as the_____ set of _____held by someone. It is also simply defined as a person's way of _____.

It determines how we think and how we interact with everyone around us.

It governs our _____, and it determines our_____ and our own personal criticism that we have _____ created within ourselves.

A mind-set can also be seen as a person's _____of life.

Research shows that positive _____, positive _____, and _____may improve your overall health.

List seven health benefits of having a positive mind-set.

1.

2.

3.

4.

5.

6.

7.

Ten Steps to Help Develop a Positive Mind-Set

1. **Take charge of yourself.**

2. **Laugh often.**

3. **Think positive.**

4. Input **control.**

5. **Gratitude.**

6. **Health.**

7. **Less worry.**

8. **Healthy relationships.**

9. **Smile often.**

10. **Embrace Life.**

Notes:

COURAGE

Courage is defined as the _____ to do something that _____ one.

Ralph Waldo Emerson said, "Whatever you do, you need courage. Whatever course you decide upon, there is always someone to tell you that you are wrong."

To map out a course of action and follow it to an end requires some of the same courage that a soldier needs."

Courage is a crucial _____ to possess in order to be _____. Contrary to what most people believe, _____ is a skill that can be _____ and _____.

Some of the benefits of courage in the workplace include

1.
2.
3.
4.
5.
6.
7.

Seven Steps to Develop Courage

1. **Dream big.**

2. **Step out of your comfort zone.**

3. **Face your fears.**

4. **Take responsibility for your actions and results.**

5. **Be ready to make mistakes.**

6. **Be independent.**

7. **Be confident.**

Notes:

CONSISTENCY

For every _____ that you make, for every goal and dream, for every plan that you have, you must be _____over time in order to be successful.

Your life today is a result of all the _____that you have made over _____. So you must take _____ to _____ these choices and make them _____; otherwise, _____choices, _____ over time, will lead to _____.

Choose **three million dollars in cash** today or a **single penny** that doubles in value every day for thirty-one days. Which would you choose?

	You	Your Friend
Day 1	$3,000,0000	$0.01
Day 5	$3,000,0000	$0.16
Day 10	$3,000,0000	$5.00
Day 20	$3,000,0000	$5,000
Day 28	$3,000,0000	$1,342,177.28
Day 31	$3,000,0000	$10,737,418.24

Consistency Tips

- Do it.
- Do it even when the going gets tough.
- Do it even when you are tired.
- Do it regardless.
- Do it every day.

Practice consistency

1. Pick one goal.

2. Write down five to seven steps to accomplish this goal.

   Step 1

   Step 2

   Step 3

   Step 4

   Step 5

   Step 6

   Step 7

   Now start doing it!

PRODUCTIVITY

Productivity is _____ the ability to get the job _____!

PLANNING

Let's examine how successful people stay productive.

What are the **specific key functions** that they perform that make them seemingly come out ahead of the rest of us more often than not?

Stephen King advocates *consistency* as one of the key attributes to success. He says, "Write every day."

Arianna Huffington, Internet publishing pioneer, advocates for *sleep.*

The late Steve Jobs had his executive team *focus* intensely on three to four projects over a period of time.

Oprah Winfrey's success is simply based on her belief that you become what you believe. Her unwavering *belief in her abilities* is what drove her to focus all of her energy on reaching her objectives. Once successful on one objective, she will then allow herself to move to the next.

A list of strategies you may adopt to improve productivity.

1. Focus on what is important.
2. Start working as soon as you get to work.
3. Wake up early.
4. Exercise three to five times a week.
5. Make a list of five distractions and work toward eliminating them.
6. Limit or schedule your social media tasking.
7. Get enough sleep.

8. Spend time with family and friends.
9. Schedule date nights with your spouse or partner.
10. Avoid procrastination.
11. Watch less TV. It's actually better to stop watching TV.
12. Don't skip breakfast.
13. Make a list of things you need to stop doing.
14. Eliminate multitasking.
15. Prioritize your work.
16. Set goals for yourself—immediate, short-, and long-term goals.
17. Plan your day ahead and write it down.
18. De-clutter your mind.
19. Learn to say no.
20. Follow doctors' orders.
21. Stay positive.
22. Think before you act.
23. Smile and laugh often.
24. Celebrate achievements.
25. Generate an emergency fund.
26. Don't argue with others.
27. Give to charity.
28. Take charge of your life. Don't let anyone be in charge of you.
29. Start a hobby.
30. Be accountable to yourself.

When it comes to productivity in a corporation, it is important to stay _____, _____ and have clearly defined and implemented strategies for measuring productivity.

Every business and organization should have strategies integrated into the business model for measuring productivity.

In the business life, a _____ plan should address all areas that may potentially affect the overall productivity of the individual or the association.

Every company or organization should have a set of _____and _____ for achieving the company's objectives.

In organizations, there are three main types of planning used in management.

1. _____ **planning** must be in line with the business goals and mission.
This deals with the _____-_____goals of the company.

2. _____ **planning,** on the other hand, deals with _____-_____ goals and specific actions necessary to achieve those goals and objectives outlined in the strategic plan.

3. _____ **planning** deals with the direct day-to-day functioning of the company itself.

PROBLEM SOLVING

Definition: It is the process of _____ through _____ of a _____ to reach a _____.

John C. Maxwell, the international leadership expert, describes problem solving, especially when it involves teamwork, as fitting the right person in the right place at the right time.

"The Wrong Person in the Wrong Place = _____.

The Wrong Person in the Right Place = _____.

The Right Person in the Wrong Place = _____.

The Right Person in the Right Place = _____.

The Right People in the Right Places = _____."

—John Maxwell.

List seven problems or challenges you are facing in your personal life and/or professional life at this time, and then go through the process of problem solving outlined in the list below.

1.

2.

3.

4.

5.

6.

7.

Problem-Solving Practice Exercise

Use this exercise to solve one of the problems that you are dealing with at this time.

1. Identify

   a. the problem.

   b. the cause.

   c. the solutions.

   d. the plan.

2. Implement the plan.

3. Evaluate the progress.

   Repeat the process for each problem.

TIME MANAGEMENT

Time management is the _____ or _____ of planning and exercising _____ control over the amount of _____ spent on specific activities, especially to increase effectiveness, efficiency, or productivity ...

Effective time management is the ability to **plan** and **control** how you spend the hours in your day to be able to accomplish your goals.

Poor time management can be related to poor organizational skills, procrastination, lack of self-control, and the inability to pace ourselves or set boundaries for ourselves.

According to the Mayo Clinic, time management has important health benefits such as:

- _____ stress
- _____ illness
- improve your _____ of life

Time is such a fleeting commodity!

Learn to focus your mind effectively and learn the foundation of time-management and productivity.

Think about your self-worth and make every effort to stop doing the things that would cost you less than what it takes you to do it.

Exercise.

List five projects that you *have not* completed on time. (You missed the deadline, or did you not have a deadline?)

1.

2.

3.

4.

5.

Notes:

Write a list of projects which did you not finish simply because of poor time management.

Take a close look at your list. Would any one of these projects be worth resuming? If so, make a plan and put that plan into action.

Effective Time-Management Strategies

1. You must know your _____.
2. _____your day ahead—every day. Write it down.
3. _____ priorities.
4. Tackle _____ and important jobs _____.
5. Schedule "_____" of thirty to sixty minutes when you are not to be interrupted so you can work on a major task.
6. Divide large tasks into _____ ones and then tackle them one at a time until they are all done.
7. _____ to others tasks that you are not expert in.
8. Hire a personal _____.
9. List _____ tasks together so they are completed at the same time.
10. Use idle time _____, for example to clean and organize your desk, to plan for the next day …
11. ___-_____ your desk.
12. Don't be a _____.
13. Avoid _____.
14. Limit the number of _____you have every day.
15. Learn to say_____ to tasks that are not related to your goals.
16. Learn to say no to _____.
17. Minimize _____ at work.
18. Avoid micro- _____.
19. Take a _____ when you need to. Rest so that you are not exhausted and emotionally drained.
20. Improve your _____ with a healthy lifestyle, eat healthy, and exercise regularly.

Notes:

COMMITMENT

Merriam-Webster's Collegiate Dictionary defines commitment as a
_____ **to** _____ **or** _____**something**, a promise to be
_____ to someone or something, the _____ of someone
who works very hard to do or support something.

> "Above all be of single aim; have a legitimate and useful
> purpose, and devote yourself unreservedly to it."
> —James Allen

Commitment to unity in marriage is one of the key factors that can keep a difficult institution like marriage thriving, regardless of the odds.

Lack of personal _____can lead to a _____in commitment on the job and can affect your company's _____.

The same goes for your personal life and relationships, especially in important relationship like marriage where lack of motivation can threaten one's commitment and this threatens the marriage itself.

Take action now. Evaluate your commitment to your goals and dreams and improve on it often.

List ten aspects of your life that warrant your commitment.

1.

2.

3.

4.

5.

6.

7.

8.

9.

10.

Notes:

Strategies to Empower Yourself to Stay Committed

1. Be clear about your goals and objectives.

2. Plan well and make a routine.

3. Model commitment yourself.

4. Give your employees challenging responsibilities incrementally.

5. Keep a journal of your progress.

6. Invest time and money wisely.

7. Review your work regularly.

GROWTH AND DEVELOPMENT

The *Wikipedia* online dictionary defines personal growth and development as "activities that improve _____ and _____, develop _____ and _____, build human capital, and facilitate _____ enhance quality of life and contribute to the realization of dreams and aspirations.

Working actively on your personal growth and development will _____ you and literally set you on a personal _____ process, which will improve your physical, emotional, intellectual, spiritual, professional, and financial situation.

Examples of Areas of Growth and Development

- faith
- finances
- character
- relationships
- career
- health
- attitude
- personality
- communication
- learning
- goal setting
- time management

For business owners, developing a business growth strategy provides an opportunity to ensure improved _____, greater _____ and more _____ on future plans, an exit plan if needed, and managed growth over time.

Areas of growth and development that helped my business *Grow to Success*.

- Planning new services
- Marketing and promoting
- Financial forecasting
- Developing a business growth strategy
- Utilizing customer feedback
- Ongoing education
- Exit planning

Now list five areas of growth and development that are important for you.

1.

2.

3.

4.

5.

Now make a growth and development plan of each of these areas listed and start the process.

Notes:

MARKETING

Definition: The _____, set of _____, and _____ for _____, communicating, _____, and exchanging offerings that have _____ for customers, clients, partners, and society at large.

Also, you must consider your _____. What are the things you have to think about in order to _____ yourself against the competition?

Four areas of marketing include

1. **Your product/service:** What product or service do you offer? Why is your product or service relevant?

2. **Your competition:** Who are your current competitors? What are their advantages? What are your customers worried about?

3. **Your customer:** Who are your customers? Describe your ideal customer. What motivates your ideal customer?

4. **Your modality:** What is the means to reach your ideal customer: TV, radio, Internet, face-to-face?

Make a list of ten marketing modalities.

1.

2.

3.

4.

5.

6.

7.

8.

9.

10.

KEEPING UP WITH CHANGING TIMES

Rapidly _____ technology will now determine the future _____ of most businesses.

Business owners must realize that their _____may be someone in a _____ simply working on a laptop miles away.

Entrepreneurs must _____ their _____ to focus on _____ the proper technology to find their customers.

"If you want to compete in today's_____ world, then it's _____to keep up with_____ ..."

Steps for Technology Awareness

1. Determine your _____.

2. _____the resources available to you.

3. _____the resources in order of usefulness to you.

4. _____or _____ the time to use the resources.

5. _____and train on the resources.

6. _____the technology evaluate its effectiveness.

What changes will you like to make in your business to "keep up" with technology advancement.

1.

2.

3.

4.

5.

Notes:

EMPLOYEE MANAGEMENT

Three key factors that impact employee engagement.

1. Relationship with immediate _____

2. Belief in senior _____

3. _____ in working for the company

This means that examining _____ practices is a key element in improving employee_____.

_____ - _____ and more _____ employees add significant _____to your customers and hence to your business.

Employee _____ is one of the greatest _____ for employees.

Discipline and _____ are key factors that help maintain _____ among employees in the workplace.

Follow through with enforcing the rules, lead with a compliment and lead by example, and don't always point out the problems.

Ways You Can Boost Your Employee Satisfaction

1.

2.

3.

Tips on Improving Your Employee Productivity

1. Ensure adequate new employee _____.
2. Provide meaningful _____.
3. Provide your employees adequate _____ to perform their jobs.
4. Train employees on a _____ work _____.
5. Design employee _____.
6. Keep employees and managers _____.
7. Identify areas that need _____.
8. Identify areas for employee _____.
9. Keep your employees _____ and _____ about new products.
10. Share _____ data.
11. Allow some _____ with work hours.
12. Train employees on how to _____ difficult _____.
13. Invest in formal _____ programs.
14. Model the _____ you want to see in your employees.

Notes:

PERSEVERANCE

To be successful, you must persevere. You must continue to do the things that work and develop them. At the same time, you must be brave and bold enough to stop doing the things that don't work.

Perseverance or tenacity, steadfastness, is defined in Merriam-Webster's Collegiate Dictionary as continued _____ to do or _____ something despite _____, _____, or _____.

To achieve personal success, one must be _____ and _____ regardless of all the obstacles that may come against us that may want to slow us down.

List seven "perseverance lessons."

1. Practice makes "_____."
2. Giving up is not an _____.
3. Be flexible only for long enough to _____ the course.
4. _____ are part of the process.
5. Be careful with _____.
6. Get _____.
7. Get out of your _____ zone.

LEADERSHIP

Leadership has been described as "a _____ by which a person _____ others toward the _____ of a common goal.

A leader should be _____ to place themselves in the fire of ever _____ demands, develop _____, strong _____ and embody the character of complete _____ to the purpose and the determination to keep on keeping on.

Think about the ten top qualities of a good leader listed in the book. Write down a list of leadership qualities that you possess.

1.

2.

3.

4.

5.

6.

7.

Remember leadership requires personal strength and development.

One of the key qualities of being a great leader is to have the capability to _____effectively with others. By practicing active _____, paying attention to body _____, and developing social _____, you will certainly grow and develop your leadership skills.

Think about a great leader that you admire and respect. Briefly explain why.

Notes:

PERSONAL IMPROVEMENT

Self-improvement   is   described   in   *Wikipedia*   as
"self-_____improvement—_____, _____, or
_____." Meaning that it is by your own _____ and efforts
that your _____ and _____ improve.

No matter where you are in _____, no matter your _____ level,
your personal sense of _____, you have room for _____.

Take inventory of yourself and identify areas that you need to improve.

Write down five areas you need to improve in your life.

1.

2.

3.

4.

5.

Strategies to Stay Motivated

RELATIONSHIPS

Merriam-Webster's Collegiate Dictionary defines relationships as the way in which_____ or _____people, groups, countries, etc. _____to, _____ toward, and _____with each other.

The relationships we _____, and how we_____ with the _____ we come in _____ with, speaks of who we are.

Name three types of relationships.

1.

2.

3.

Now think about the close relationships you have in your life and evaluate the value these relationships add to your life.

Notes:

FAITH AND MOTIVATION

Staying motivated and having faith in your dream will set and keep you on the path to success.

Ten Steps to Stay Motivated

1. _____ and _____ big.
2. _____ your goal.
3. _____ and study.
4. _____ out of your _____ zone.
5. _____ off the negativity.
6. Make a _____ and put your _____ into _____.
7. _____ your achievements.
8. Be persistent.
9. Believe in yourself.
10. Be consistent.

"Now *faith* is the substance of things hoped for, the evidence of things not seen" (Hebrews 11:1 King James Version).

Faith is defined in Merriam-Webster's Collegiate Dictionary as an _____ to _____ or a person.

Other definitions include _____, fidelity to one's _____, sincerity of _____, belief, and trust in and loyalty to God or in the traditional doctrines of a religion.

So you see, the definition of faith is not exclusive to religion. It simply specifies the belief in something intangible without physical evidence.

Prayer is one of the ways to feed your faith.

Prayer is not only asking _____ when we want something.

It is in fact _____ with the Almighty Father.

We _____with God because He is our father, friend, and soul mate. And like in conversation, it is not always about _____ but _____ too. It comes out of love, faith, and belief.

Make a list of ten prayer requests.

1.

2.

3.

4.

5.

6.

7.

8.

9.

10.

Notes:

RECREATION

Merriam-Webster's Collegiate Dictionary defines _____ as something people do to _____or have _____; _____ done for _____; _____ of strength and spirits after work; a means of refreshment or diversion.

In order to be _____, one must train oneself to find a _____ between work and recreation.

To be more_____, learn to take _____ away from work and _____'s obligations so that you can _____ your energies.

Name five positive outcomes of increased physical activity.

1.
2.
3.
4.
5.

Tips to help you add recreation to your schedule.

- planning
- time management
- eliminating unnecessary activities
- not waiting
- learning to say no

Make a list of recreational activities that you like and make a plan to start or continue these activities.

Notes:

HEALTHY LIFESTYLE CHANGES

The World Health Organization (WHO) defines health as a state of complete _____, _____, and _____well-being, not simply just the absence of disease.
(https://apps.who.int/aboutwho/en/definition.html)

You make every effort to put yourself in a place of optimum health by taking care of your body, your emotions, and your relationships. Without good health you will not go very far.

Note:

- Adopting a healthy lifestyle is certainly not easy.
- Incorporate one step at a time.
- Change will not happen overnight.
- It will involve dedication and consistency.
- It will involve you taking responsibility.

List three benefits of a healthy lifestyle.

1.

2.

3.

Steps to Take toward a Healthy Lifestyle

1. Change your _____ .
2. Set _____long and short term.
3. Set up an _____system.
4. _____ three to four times a week.
5. Stop _____.
6. Eat ___ to ___small healthy meals daily.
7. Work toward a health _____.
8. Know your _____ .
9. Reduce _____.
10. Plan your _____.

Notes:

Wellness

Wellness is generally used to mean a healthy _____ of the mind, body, and spirit that results in an overall feeling of well-being.

Wellness is achieved by _____ and _____to practice relevant health and wellness actions on a long-term basis.

Strategies to Help You Accomplish Your Wellness Goals

1. Eat _____.

2. Exercise _____.

3. Manage _____.

4. Balance your _____.

5. Get regular _____.

6. _____ well.

7. Improve your_____ and _____health.

Notes: